Ritalin Is Not the Answer

David B. Stein, Ph.D.

Foreword by Peter R. Breggin, M.D.

Ritalin Is Not the Answer

A Drug-Free, Practical Program for Children Diagnosed with ADD or ADHD

Jossey-Bass Publishers
San Francisco

Jossey-Bass books and products are available through most bookstores.
To contact Jossey-Bass directly, call (888) 378-2537, fax to (800) 605-2665,
or visit our website at www.josseybass.com.

Substantial discounts on bulk quantities of Jossey-Bass books are available
to corporations, professional associations, and other organizations. For details
and discount information, contact the special sales department at Jossey-Bass.

Manufactured in the United States of America.

Library of Congress Cataloging-in-Publication Data
Stein, David B.
    Ritalin is not the answer : a drug-free, practical program for
children diagnosed with ADD or ADHD / David B. Stein, Foreword by
Peter R. Breggin. — 1st ed.
      p. cm.
    Includes bibliographical references (p.   ) and index.
    ISBN 0-7879-4514-5 (cloth : acid-free paper)
    1. Attention-deficit hyperactivity disorder—Alternative
treatment.   I. Breggin, Peter Roger, 1936– II. Title.
    RJ506.H9 S68 1999
    618.92'858906—dc21
                              98-25535
                              CIP

FIRST EDITION
PB Printing 10 9 8 7 6 5

CONTENTS

FOREWORD

Today millions of parents are trying to deal with warnings or complaints from teachers about the behavior of their children. Many other parents are finding themselves stressed by the challenge of raising children in the modern world.

What do you do when the teacher says your child's behavior is disrupting the class or your child has a problem paying attention? What do you do at home when you cannot calm your children down or get them to pay attention to anything you have to say?

As psychologist David Stein describes, too many parents have given up in frustration after trying their best to control their children by "coaching, promoting, suggesting, coaxing, reminding, and warning," as suggested by currently popular behavioral treatments. Every parent in distress has probably tried all of these things, often to no avail. In confusion and frustration, these parents may turn to more ominous threats or harmful spankings, which they end up regretting afterward. Being a parent is truly the most difficult job in the world.

Modern biological psychiatry has a pat answer. Your child has ADHD and needs medication. It's an easy solution to the hardest job there is—but it's a solution that does not address your child's real needs. It's an answer that doesn't help you become a more effective and loving parent.

Diagnosing and drugging children makes them feel blamed and stigmatized, ultimately lowering their self-esteem. It encourages them to believe that they cannot learn to control their own behavior without resorting to drugs.

Stein points out that stimulant drugs act as a chemical restraint. As I describe in my book *Talking Back to Ritalin*, the behavior of children taking the drug can be subdued or suppressed for a few weeks or months without improving academic performance and without there being any long-term benefit. Stein is right when he says that drugs cannot help a child learn to think.

Stimulant drugs can also cause many adverse effects, including addiction and withdrawal symptoms, growth retardation, and a worsening of the very symptoms they are supposed to treat, including hyperactivity and inattention.

When professionals do attempt to help parents take new approaches to their children, they often prescribe simplistic behavioral modification techniques. A child may be exposed to systematic rewards, sometimes including tokens or happy-face stickers. But these methods usually generate further conflicts between the parent and child. The youngster sees the process as one more manipulation. As Stein realizes, currently available behavior modification techniques don't help parents develop genuinely better relationships with their children, they don't help parents improve their parenting skills, and they don't help children learn to think rationally for themselves.

The combination of medication and the current simplistic behavioral techniques disempowers parents. It leaves them dependent on professionals for drug prescriptions and behavioral programs without giving parents the principles and specific approaches they need for helping their children.

Parents today need better ideas and approaches. They need to believe in themselves as parents. They need the psychological tools for retaking responsibility for their children. They need to focus on the development of *their own skills* as parents. By increasing their own skills, parents can help their children grow into more self-disciplined, rational beings. *Ritalin Is Not the Answer* makes a major contribution toward helping parents learn to be more effective in raising their children—especially in helping children learn to think rationally.

Stein is very clear that in most cases children labeled ADHD have nothing whatsoever wrong with them. He tells us, "First, I see these children as completely normal. They are quite capable of behaving, attending, and thinking." They are *normal, healthy* children.

Some of these children are being exposed to confusing and frustrating situations at school or at home. Unrealistic or contradictory expectations are being placed on them. Others have not been given the tools they need to control their own behavior and to focus their attention, even under the best of circumstances. For parents who want to help their children develop their intellectual capacities, including self-control and concentration, this book provides a valuable approach.

Stein also appreciates the adage "It takes a village to raise a child." He knows that many people can and should be involved in caretaking and bringing up our children. Consistent with my own clinical practice, he involves all caretakers in his training program, including grandparents and older siblings. As a professor, he teaches the same techniques to teachers.

Finally, I want to confirm Stein's emphasis on loving relationships. Our children are gifts—treasures—whose lives we hold in our hands. We must also hold them in our hearts. This book will help empower you as a parent and, in the process, help you create a more loving, yet disciplined, relationship with your children. Your

To my wonderful children
Kevin, Alex, and Heidi
with all my love.

PREFACE

Ritalin is not a drug to be trifled with. It is an amphetamine. It is a "gateway" drug that is more powerful than marijuana and can trigger an addiction in a child from which there may be no return. Ritalin has dangerous short-term side effects; that is, the effects appear within weeks or months after initiating the drug. It also has long-term side effects, about which research is lacking. And yet each year Ritalin—or some related drug—is being prescribed for millions of children as a quick fix for not behaving well or for not doing their schoolwork with care.

Ritalin is prescribed for children who allegedly have ADD or ADHD (attention deficit disorder or attention deficit hyperactive disorder)—diseases that cause poor attention and inappropriate, hyperactive behavior. Viewed as disease, the core of treatment is medication: Ritalin. The behavioral programs for ADD and ADHD that have been developed to date are designed to merely augment treatment with Ritalin. Because these children are viewed as sick, handicapped, and unable to function on their own, behavioral treatments are designed to assist ADD and ADHD children by coaching, prompting, suggesting, coaxing, reminding, and warning.

However, in this book you will learn that these children don't have a disease and that these behavioral treatments actually contribute to making ADD and ADHD children dependent and helpless. Many behavioral programs, in addition to making a few basic suggestions, lean heavily on a technique called a token economy in which symbolic tokens (such as check marks, stars, happy faces) are given as rewards when children follow the behavioral rules posted on a chart. When enough tokens are accumulated, the child can purchase a treat or a fun activity. I view the token economy as an abnormal model for raising a child. Also, it includes many prompts and reminders that further contribute to these children's helplessness.

Ritalin works. I can't argue that it doesn't. In fact, it works for anybody, not just ADD and ADHD kids. It drugs you. It produces a subdued feeling and a calming effect. But in giving it to our children, we are making them drugged persons.

It is understandable that we want to curtail the behavior of a child who is disrupting the learning environment for other children or becoming a terror at home. However, *Ritalin is chemical restraint.* The idea that ADD and ADHD children are diseased and that Ritalin is the only solution is scientifically unsound and morally wrong. Putting millions of children on Ritalin or any other amphetamine is a dangerous trend. How can we wage a war on drugs in this country when we are putting these same chemicals into children's bodies under the guise of treatment? This must stop! A comprehensive behavioral approach that is totally chemical-free is needed as an alternative. This book presents such an approach.

THE CAREGIVERS' SKILLS PROGRAM

You will be introduced to the Caregivers' Skills Program, which is designed to make ADD and ADHD children behave correctly, function independently, pay attention, and actually think and problem solve without medication. You, the adults who care for these children, will be thoroughly trained in all the skills needed to raise healthy and happy children.

As a practitioner and researcher, I've developed this program over twenty-five years with hundreds of children. The techniques require no charts and tokens. Interactions between caregiver and child are normal and healthy. Children are not viewed as diseased but as normal kids who can function with proper incentives and control techniques.

In this book you'll learn in more detail about the risks and dangers of Ritalin, the reasons attentional disorders are not diseases, the ways behavioral methods actually perpetuate ADD and ADHD problems, and ways to improve the behavior and thinking patterns of these children—without using drugs.

ACKNOWLEDGMENTS

I wish to thank a number of special people who have helped in the preparation of this book. Joyce Trent has spent countless hours in manuscript preparation and editing. I couldn't have done this without her. Her patience and fortitude are heroic. Joanne Stanley, before her retirement, preceded Joyce. Tammy Williams and Missy Johns helped collect and organize the overwhelming volume of literature on attentional disorders. My editor and friend Laurie Rosin put her heart and soul into the preparation of this book. Her faith, support, and encouragement helped so much to keep me going when I was up late at night and early the next morning doing my work.

I give special thanks to Faith Beattie, who cared for my children during work hours. She loves them and they love her. She has been a godsend. Another special person in the lives of my children is Janie Singleton, who was the first teacher each of my boys had. She made their introduction to education a joy. My children, out of love, have actively stayed in touch with her throughout the years.

My friend and colleague Ed Smith encouraged and motivated me. Don Stuart spent valuable time in his busy schedule, while he was vice president of the college, to edit the manuscript. Pharmacologist Steven La Haye helped with the drug research. My pastor, James Flamming, who is a remarkable person, helped keep me spiritually centered throughout the arduous periods of isolation needed to complete my work. I am grateful for the phone calls and expressions of support from my dearest friends, Barry Kudlowitz, Laura Birdsong, and Ira Rakoff.

Special thanks to my agent, Jeff Herman, who stuck with me through thick and thin, and to Alan Rinzler, executive editor at Jossey-Bass Publishers, for making this book not only possible but much better.

DAVID B. STEIN

Ritalin Is Not the Answer

1

WHAT ARE
WE DOING
TO OUR
CHILDREN?

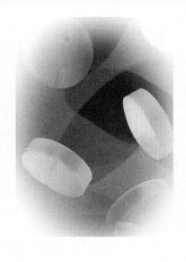

In this chapter I hope to open your eyes with some thought-provoking scenarios. Then I'll briefly review the growing anti-Ritalin movement. Finally, I'll explain why currently available behavioral methods are insufficient in treating attentional disorders and why I have developed a new and more comprehensive treatment called the Caregivers' Skills Program.

Let's begin our journey with a little exercise in imagination. I will describe two scenarios, and I would like you to try to picture each scene as vividly as you can and focus very carefully on your emotional reactions.

THE PUSHER

It's 10 A.M. The temperature is a comfortable 70 degrees and the air smells fresh. You decide to go for a slow stroll and approach the schoolyard of Jane Doe Elementary School. Something unusual catches your eye. The schoolyard is empty except for a large group of children clustered near a windowless corner. You notice that the group is made up mostly of boys.

Something doesn't seem right. Quietly you enter the yard and walk up behind the group. The children appear to be between the ages of seven and ten, and you notice that they are surrounding a man with their hands outstretched. He is a rough-looking type of guy. His arms are covered with tattoos; his hair is long and greasy. He is dressed in jeans and a dirty, dark-blue, sleeveless T-shirt. In this man's right hand you see a large bottle filled with pills, and suddenly you realize he's shaking pills into the hands of the children! He's saying, "Yeah, man. Take these and you feel real good. They make you do good in school, too. Then everyone goin' to like you. Trust me. I'll be here every day to bring you some more and take real good care of you."

You push several of the children aside as you walk up to the man and grab the bottle. It's marked SPEED.

How would you feel? What would your perceptions be? What would you do? Hit the man? Yell at him? Or you might rush to a phone to call the police.

Now let's run through our second scenario.

THE NURSE

It is 10 A.M. The temperature is a comfortable 70 degrees and the air smells fresh. You decide to go for a slow stroll to visit your son Tommy's class at Jane Doe Elementary School.

Upon entering the building you head to the main office to register. As you approach the office you notice a long line of children who appear to be between seven and ten years of age. Most of them are boys. At the head of the line is the school nurse, neatly dressed in her starched white uniform. She is shaking the contents of several little brown bottles filled with pills into the hands of each child. She is saying, "Now take your medicine. It will make you feel so much better. It will help you do better work in your classes, and you won't get in trouble with your teachers any more. Your doctor and I know what is best for you. You can trust us." You peek over the shoulder of the nurse and notice the bottles are marked RITALIN.

Well, how do you feel now? Do I make my point? Do we as parents, educators, and doctors realize what we are doing? We are shoving some of the most highly addicting substances—amphetamines—down the throats of our children in the name of treatment.

The basic difference between the two scenes is the identity of the pusher. The long line of children is not a product of my imagination. It is a reality that takes place every day in almost every elementary school in the country. Visit a few schools and you will witness this about ten in the morning during medication time. The number of children waiting in line will astonish you.

Examine, if you will, the great paradox or contradiction in American society today. On the one hand we are fighting the evils and perils of drugs among the young. On the other hand, we are dishing out these very same drugs to them as so-called medicines. Ritalin, Dexedrine, Adderall, Benzedrine, and most other drugs given to children in the name of treatment for attentional disorders are listed by the federal government as Schedule II drugs. This means they have such great addictive potential that physicians' prescriptions for them must be monitored and controlled. This is the same category of drugs in which opium, morphine, and cocaine are listed. Cylert, a less addicting Schedule IV drug, has recently been implicated in liver failure and is being prescribed less and less.

Let me make a crucial point. There is absolutely no way we can tell which child has the potential to become a drug addict or an alcoholic. No psychological test can do this. No medical test can do this. But any drug in the category with the amphetamines can trigger an addiction process that, once started, probably cannot be readily reversed. Someone has to tell me why parents and professionals are willing to take this risk with children!

The Danger of Addiction

Ms. Jones is currently one of my patients. She is a forty-two-year-old single mother of two boys, ages nineteen and eleven. She is seeing me for treatment of depression and guilt. Her oldest son, Kyle, is in jail serving a five-year sentence for possessing and selling drugs. He is a heroin addict.

When Kyle was eight he was diagnosed as having ADD (attention deficit disorder). He was making B's in school, but the teachers felt that he could do so much better if only he would pay more careful attention. It seemed he daydreamed a lot. At home, however, he would sit for hours squinting into his microscope. He had a rock collection and loved to make shavings in order to examine the crystal formations. His rock collection was diligently categorized and well organized. He was actually a very bright and well-contented child. None of this information deterred his teachers. They insisted he should be doing better.

A team meeting was called. The team was made up of the school nurse, Kyle's teachers, the school psychologist, the guidance counselor, the assistant principal, and, of course, the mother. It was decided that Kyle should be tested by the school psychologist and that the team would reconvene once the findings were made. It was found that Kyle had a very high level of intelligence. His mother was told that he tested at the "very superior" intellectual level. There was no evidence of learning disabilities. But he tested positive for ADD.

Ms. Jones asked the school psychologist how Kyle could spend so many hours over his rock collection, sometimes not glancing up for hours. The psychologist replied that ADD was a selective disease. Children who have it can pay attention to activities that provide immediate reinforcement. Even though Ms. Jones remained puzzled by this answer, she did not wish to be rude so she did not pursue the issue further.

The team emphatically recommended that Kyle be started on Ritalin. Ms. Jones requested a chance to discuss this with her family doctor. The doctor felt the recommendation might be a good idea and besides it couldn't hurt. He wrote the prescription immediately and Ms. Jones dutifully complied.

Kyle's grades did not improve very much, but the teacher reported he was paying much better attention. He was kept on the medication for the next several years. Kyle came to believe that he needed the medicine in order to continue to perform well in school. He wanted to stay on the medication. The school authorities and the family doctor concurred.

In his early teens, Kyle began experimenting with other drugs that were readily available at school. He began smoking pot and taking any type of pills he could get his hands on. At age fifteen he discovered heroin. It was all downhill from there.

In listening to the details of this case it immediately occurred to me that Kyle is an auditory type of learner. In other words he learns best by listening and needs very little eye contact with what is being taught. That is just his style of learning. He was listening carefully but only needed to glance at his work. The authorities interpreted this to mean he was not paying attention.

Ms. Jones was bullied by the system into starting her child on an amphetamine. She trusted the teachers, the school psychologist, the nurse, and her doctor. And in addition, the poor woman had no idea what Ritalin really was. The price she paid is both tragic and inexcusable.

By the way, Ms. Jones, while seeing me as a patient, was told by her younger son's teacher that he too had ADD. Again the teacher recommended that the school psychologist test him for the possibility that he needs to use Ritalin. Ms. Jones said that if anyone went near her child with any of these drugs she'd sue. I tested her son's intelligence level and he scored at the very top of the test.

DOCTORS' CONFUSION ABOUT RITALIN

Does Ritalin work? Yes! But, no one knows for certain exactly how. Some say that it increases the activity of what is called the inhibitory center of the brain. This is believed to be a tiny part of the brain that helps us to slow down or stop a behavior, but there is no proof for this supposition. This theory is only a guess (a hypothesis), not a fact. In addition, Ritalin does improve alertness, but only when first used. All stimulants do. However, Ritalin does these things for all people, not just attentional-hyperactive children. I believe it produces these effects because it makes us high, calms us down, and makes us feel good. Because it is a stimulant drug, far more powerful than caffeine, it perks us up and makes us more alert.

So what's the problem? Isn't it a safe drug? No, it is not! It has many dangerous and risky properties such as the potential for addiction, short-term side effects, and long-term side effects.

In the next chapter I'll discuss the issue of side effects in more detail. However, for now I want to briefly address the addiction issue. Physicians often tell parents that the fear of addiction is unfounded. Try the following exercise:

Call your family doctor's office and make an appointment for yourself. When the doctor comes in to examine you and asks what you are there for, tell him you want to lose some weight and you read that amphetamines are excellent drugs to reduce appetite (one of the side effects of amphetamines). Firmly insist that the doctor start you immediately on a prescription for any of the amphetamines, and be sure to state clearly that you want to stay on the medication for two, three, or even more years. Watch your doctor's reaction and response.

Your doctor will tell you that under no circumstances would he do such a thing. He will tell you that these are dangerous drugs that you shouldn't fool around with. He'll tell you about the side effects such as insomnia, nervousness, irritable stomach, hypertension—

perhaps even feelings of paranoia—and so forth. Then, I promise you, he will say, "Besides, these drugs are too easy to get addicted to, and it would be unethical to prescribe them in such a fashion, especially for so many years!"

Think about this. Doctors will not prescribe these drugs to you, a responsible adult, but they readily load your children down with them. Not only does this dichotomous thinking on the part of physicians seem to elude them but they are prescribing these drugs at an ever-increasing rate. Almost one million children are being given a prescription for Ritalin each year, and another million are given alternative amphetamines.

THE GROWING ANTI-RITALIN MOVEMENT

In the last several years a number of changes have occurred in the way we view attentional disorders and in the way we treat them. As we shall see in this section, more and more doctors are no longer viewing attentional disorders as diseases. In addition, there is mounting evidence against the safety of putting Ritalin and related drugs into the bodies of children. If there is no disease underlying the behaviors and if the medications are truly risky—perhaps not even necessary—the development of more effective behavioral treatments becomes more essential. More effective treatment without drugs is what this book is about.

Let's look at the changes in thought about attentional disorders being the result of an underlying disease.

THE DISEASE ERA

In the 1980s psychologists began to turn their attention to the treatment of attentional disorders. I call this the Barkley Disease Era, because it was psychologist Russell Barkley who led the way to the popular belief that the disorders were incurable diseases. No evidence to support the disease concept existed then and it remains unsubstantiated to this day. However, the symptoms of this so-called disease, according to Barkley, could be controlled by a combination of Ritalin and behavioral treatments.

The movement took off with Barkley's (1981) book, *Hyperactive Children: A Handbook for Diagnosis and Treatment*. The book offered a few behavioral suggestions, including a technique that had been around for some time called a token economy. The token economy involves giving a child some type of symbolic reward, such as check marks on a chart or poker chips, after a "good" behavior. When enough tokens are accumulated, the child may purchase a treat or a privilege.

Barkley later found support for his disease theory in the research of Alan J. Zametkin (Zametkin, Liebenauer, Gitzgerald, and King, 1993), a medical doctor whose research focused on scanning the pattern of cell metabolism in the brain using a machine called a PET (position emission tomography) scan. Metabolism is the energy emitted by the brain cells when consuming glucose, and the PET scan can measure metabolism in areas of the brain that give off low-energy emissions and compare them to areas with high-energy emissions. Zametkin claimed to have found different patterns in ADHD children than in normal children. However, his research was not originally conducted on children but on adults who were believed to have been ADHD when they were children. Furthermore, researchers reviewing his studies refuted the conclusions he drew and found flaws in his methods of analysis (Breggin, 1998). Unfortunately, both Barkley and Zametkin persisted in their claims. A couple of years later Zametkin came forth and admitted that in follow-up research he could not substantiate his own earlier findings, as they were described in Breggin's (1998) book, *Talking Back to Ritalin*.

Zametkin and Barkley have since collaborated on numerous PET scan studies and continue to make the same claims. They seem to ignore the very basic fact that PET scans are not, at this time, an accurate device (Sedvall, 1992; Mayberg, 1998). To make claims of the discovery of a disease when using a machine that does not yield precise readings is poor science. Remember that their claim has paved the way for two million children being placed on amphetamines.

After Zametkin's first studies appeared, researchers claimed that other areas of the brain and nervous system were implicated as "the disease" causing the inattentive and overacting misbehaviors. Claims of malfunction have been attributed to brainstem dysfunction, caudate nucleus dysfunction, corpus callosum abnormalities, the dopamine hypothesis, folic acid abnormalities, frontal lobe dysfunction, imbalances of brain chemicals, prefrontal cortex dysfunction, and serum lipid imbalances.

I include this scientific-sounding list to show you how out of hand things have become in the attempt to find an elusive disease that causes children to not pay attention and move around a lot.

DOCTORS REFUTE DISEASE THEORIES

Well-known pediatric neurologists such as Gerald Golden (1974) and Fred Braughman, as well as Breggin, have refuted all claims that disease is present. Braughman, in a 1997 newspaper article, writes, "In plain words, ADD [and ADHD] is an expensive, elaborately woven illusion of a disease—not a disease at all" (pp. 1–2). Even agencies of the federal government have weighed in on the matter. The Drug Enforcement Administration stated in 1996 that no "specific neurological lesion or deficit" has been found and that studies making such claims cannot be replicated by other scientists.

Did you know that in psychology and psychiatry there is no agreed upon definition for the term "disease"? Not having a precise definition opens the door for anyone to label the slightest or subtlest of physiological (body) differences a disease. What one doctor calls a disease, another may interpret as not being a disease. There is a wide range for the diversity of normal human behaviors, under which lies an equally wide range of physiological differences. It is important, therefore, that psychologists and psychiatrists not loosely use the term disease, as some are currently doing, because the consequences mean putting powerful chemicals into the bodies of our children.

HOW A DISEASE OR NO-DISEASE DIAGNOSIS DETERMINES TREATMENT

The assumption that disease exists is important because it has major implications for the way we approach treatment. If we assume there is a disease, treatment takes the direction of medication coupled with the assistance of a few behavioral helping aids. If we assume no disease, medication isn't really necessary and well-designed behavioral methods should work alone.

In addition, if children are assumed to have a disease, they cannot help themselves; it follows that behavioral methods should be designed to assist them in every way possible, as opposed to making them function correctly and completely on their own. My methods are designed to treat them as normal kids who can function quite well with proper behavioral intervention. But before we consider my recommendations, let's take a closer look at recent changes in treatment.

THE MOVE AWAY FROM RITALIN

Ritalin and other amphetamines have been viewed as safe for over twenty years. However, new evidence is calling this point of view into question. The short-term side effects—those appearing within a day or several days after beginning Ritalin or related drugs—have been documented. I review these in more detail in the next chapter but they include irregular heartbeat, rapid heartbeat, elevation of blood pressure, nausea, and sleeplessness. Usually doctors handle the emergence of short-term side effects by a trial-and-error process of switching to another drug. Of even more concern are long-term side effects that may take years to show up and are often irreversible.

Only scant research on long-term effects exists, but the little that does is cause for concern. First and foremost are concerns about triggering the addiction process. Ritalin or any amphetamine is a more dangerous gateway or starter drug than marijuana. More and more children aged ten to fourteen abuse Ritalin as a street drug (International Narcotics Control Board, 1996). Ritalin and closely related drugs are amphetamines, which are acknowledged in almost every text on drugs as the most addicting category of all drugs.

In addition, for over twenty years Ritalin and related drugs have caused concern about normal physical growth in children. It is well documented that normal growth is stunted in children while on Ritalin, or related drugs. Once the child is taken off the drug, a growth spurt follows. Weiner (1982) stated that there is no way to determine if these children ever catch up to the size they could have been. If a child's growth, including head and brain growth, is interrupted during critical developmental years, then the question remains about damage that may only surface twenty or thirty years later. No research exists on this issue. My common sense tells me that it can't possibly be good to interfere with children's normal growth patterns.

Ritalin and other drugs may also cause permanent brain damage (Giedd and others, 1994; Nasrallah and others, 1986; Mathieu, Ferron, Dewar, and Reader, 1989). Another study (Auci, 1997) indicates that Ritalin may interfere with a healthy, functioning immune system. All of this points to the need for better and more effective behavioral treatments.

CHANGES IN BEHAVIORAL TREATMENTS

To understand the evolution of the behavioral treatments, we must understand a basic behavioral concept, which can be illustrated as follows:

Preceding Stimuli → Responses → Consequent Stimuli

The preceding stimuli are environmental events that cue or trigger a behavior to occur, such as a red light warning you to stop the car. The responses are the behaviors. In attentional disorders we typically focus on responses such as impulsivity, pushing, not sitting still, not paying attention, or interrupting. The consequent stimuli are the environmental events that follow the behaviors, such as rewards (reinforcements) and punishments.

During the Barkley Disease Era the predominant focus of behavioral treatments has been on the preceding stimuli. Because certain children are considered sick—they have a disease—it follows that they need lots of help. Thus we've seen books that advocate "helping" the child with an abundance of social and environmental cueing and prompting (preceding stimuli) to direct the child in performing the desired behaviors. These helping methods include giving more individual attention in the classroom, helping children with their homework, reminding them to think about how they should behave before entering any place, tutoring them individually, coaching them when organizing their schoolwork, and coaching them to stop and think before doing a behavior. Also needed: lots and lots of reminding by adults and lots and lots of warnings before children earn a bad consequence. Token economies provide lots of visual cueing using charts, to-do lists, and physical tokens, such as poker chips. These cues serve as reminders that interfere with children's learning to remember on their own what they are to do.

A NEW METHOD

My approach is quite different. First, I see ADD and ADHD children as completely normal. They are quite capable of behaving, attending, and thinking. The problem is a thinking problem. They don't think or pay attention to what they are doing, especially in activities they simply don't like, such as schoolwork. I will discuss the thinking problems in more detail in Chapter Two.

In this book I decrease or eliminate the emphasis on preceding stimuli—the reminding, the coaxing, the helping, the warning. All these techniques contribute to making mental invalids of our children. Using them makes children mentally dependent on helpers. Excessive helping, with no teaching to function on their own, makes children thoroughly dependent and totally helpless for the rest of their lives. This is exactly what the current behavioral approaches are doing.

The current approaches make parents into ever-present reminder machines, creating what is called cognitive (thinking) dependency in these children. They can't think or function without someone constantly reminding them. Is it any wonder that we have to continue coaching them and filling them with drugs well into adolescence and adult life? We haven't taught them to function, so when all this excessive assistance is removed and the drugs are stopped, they can't make it on their own. This is not because of some mysterious disease that no one seems to be able to find but because we failed to make them stand on their own two feet and learn how to function. Psychologist Claude Steiner (1974) writes that making children helpless and dependent invalids is the worst of all things parents can do to their children.

Remember the play *The Miracle Worker* about how caregiver Annie Sullivan taught Helen Keller to communicate and behave like a human being instead of an animal? This is considered the first documented behavior modification case. Annie Sullivan knew Helen was normal and could function. She isolated Helen from the pampering of her family and made her function. The results produced one of America's greatest heroines. We can do for the ADD and ADHD children what Annie Sullivan did for Helen Keller.

A basic premise of this book is that these children are normal and can function. I focus on how we can effectively control the consequent stimuli by teaching them and requiring them to behave themselves and to pay attention when they are supposed to. This book is a rigorous, systematic, sensible parenting approach.

CHANGES IN PARENT ADVICE BOOKS

Because the way we view attentional disorders as diseases or not diseases has changed, and the evidence of the risks associated with the drugs has increased, the advice given in books for parents has changed in orientation as well.

1980 to 1992

During this period, attentional disorders were viewed as diseases and the medications to treat them were considered safe. Starting with Barkley's book in 1981 and a number of books that followed, treatment consisted of a strong recommendation to use Ritalin or related drugs coupled with the type of behavioral methods in which lots of help is given to a child who is viewed as sick, diseased, and therefore helpless.

1992 to 1997

More recently, the titles of books began to demonstrate the growing concerns about Ritalin. These include *Do We Really Need Ritalin?* (Wright, 1997), *Beyond Ritalin* (Garber, Garber, and Spezman, 1996), *The Ritalin-Free Child* (Hunter, 1995), *Ritalin-Free Kids* (Reichenberg-Ullman and Ullman, 1996), and *No More Ritalin* (Block, 1996). These books review the mounting evidence of the risks of drug therapy and express a growing negative point of view toward the use of these drugs.

However, the books do not readily acknowledge the evidence against the disease concept. Therefore, the behavioral approaches in these books still offer the methods I cited earlier in which the child is viewed as diseased and helpless. Prominent psychiatrists and psychologists such as L. E. Arnold and others (1994), Phil Kendall

(1987), and Peter Breggin (1998) point out that these methods have not been very successful.

1998—A New Era

Breggin's book, *Talking Back to Ritalin* (1998), makes a strong and thorough argument against the disease concept for attentional disorders and an equally powerful argument against the use of Ritalin and related drugs. Breggin also questions the effectiveness of currently available behavioral methods.

Other writers and researchers such as Kendall and Braswell (1993) note the limited success with current methods and point to the need for developing a comprehensive parenting approach designed specifically for ADD and ADHD treatment.

Each of these writers sees ADD and ADHD as manifestations of cognitive (thinking) problems in normal children who don't think or pay attention to what they are doing. They especially see problems in the motivation of these children to behave and perform well in school.

A NEW MODEL FOR PARENTING THE ADD OR ADHD CHILD WITHOUT MEDICATION

When I see ADD or ADHD children as patients, I block off several sessions in order to train the parents. It's like a class. I teach and the parents take notes and ask questions. I know of no other therapist who does this. To me it always makes sense to thoroughly train the people who spend time with the children.

Parent training was introduced in the early 1970s by Wes Becker (1971) and Gerald Patterson (1971) and has proved enormously successful with most children. I have redesigned the parent-training methods specifically for ADD and ADHD children. I have devoted almost twenty-five years of practice and research to refining this approach, gradually learning what works with these children and what doesn't.

Be patient. It takes the rest of this book to teach you the specifics. What you will learn here is neither vague nor piecemeal. This is a systematic, comprehensive, nuts-and-bolts book. Everything you will learn has been practiced and refined over many years with hundreds of ADD and ADHD children.

ALTERNATIVES FOR PHYSICIANS

Physicians are trained to heal. They really want to help. They often claim that they don't have an alternative—that the only way to help these children is with drugs. Besides, parents and teachers are constantly at their throats for them to write these prescriptions. They want their disruptive kids under control immediately. Some doctors dislike doing this; many wish for an alternative.

Doctors! Here now is an alternative. Take your prescription pad and write down the title of this book. Recommend that parents (and teachers) read it each evening at bedtime. Mind-altering drugs are not the right way to teach children to learn and behave. Before putting powerful chemicals into the developing bodies of children, try my prescription first.

Parents! Stop being bullied by the system. Protect your children. Do not let the teachers, doctors, psychiatrists, or psychologists tell you that they know what is best for your child. What I present here is safe, nonaddictive, healthy, and sensible. And most important, *it works*.

In the following chapters I will dispel a number of myths surrounding this growing epidemic of attentional disorders and the monumental reliance on chemical behavior control. When finished with this book, you will have learned rigorous parenting skills to overcome your child's difficulties. What is covered in this book is not complicated, nor is it difficult to implement. However, it will require work on your part. I am not offering a quick fix. You will have to roll up your sleeves. But if you practice what you will be taught, you should see a well-behaved and motivated child. You will enjoy being with your child more and hopefully develop a closer, more loving relationship. You will develop more confidence in your parenting skills.

Typically, in my last sessions with parents, I hear, "He seems so much happier," when referring to their child. This is where I want you to be.

2

UNDERSTANDING THE MYTHS OF ATTENTIONAL DISORDERS

In this chapter we'll look at the prevalence of Ritalin use; I'll share my personal story, and we'll look at the seven myths about attentional disorders.

THE EPIDEMIC OF ADD AND ADHD AND THE GROWING USE OF RITALIN

Here's a bad joke: What's the difference between an adult and a child? The adult is on Prozac and the child is on Ritalin.

Not very funny, is it? But that now describes the situation in the United States of America. Each study or report I read indicates different figures, but it seems that somewhere between one-tenth to one-quarter of all school-age children are diagnosed as having some form of attentional disorder—attention deficit disorder (ADD) or attention deficit hyperactive disorder (ADHD). The ratio of diagnosis of boys to girls is about 5 to 1. It also seems that most of these youngsters are being treated with Ritalin or some other type of mood-altering medication.

With so many children on Ritalin, are we in the midst of an epidemic or plague? Do you wonder where this plague came from and why it is spreading so fast? Are ADD and ADHD caused by a highly contagious airborne virus or resistant bacteria? If it were a disease, could it completely disappear—be cured—solely with behavioral management? Is it genetic? But if we parents are transmitting an attentional disorder to our children, why didn't we suffer from it when we were kids?

MY PERSONAL EXPERIENCE

I'm a parent, just like most of you. My children live with my ex-wife. My older son, Alex, now age twelve, was diagnosed as ADD several years ago and put on Ritalin. My younger son, Kevin, now age ten, was diagnosed as ADHD and put on Cylert (similar to Ritalin) and then Tofranil, an antidepressant, because of difficulties with sleeplessness and nightmares.

Besides being a dad, I am a practicing clinical psychologist and a college professor of psychology. I teach courses in child psychopathology and behavior modification that require me to remain up to date on the diagnosis and treatment of childhood disorders. I also teach a course in psychopharmacology, which focuses on the effects of drugs on behavior, the body, and the nervous system. My research and writings center on the diagnosis and treatment of attentional, behavioral, and motivational problems in children. So I knew the long-term psychological and physiological risks of these drugs. This added to my fears.

Kevin's heart developed an irregular beat and was spiking at over two hundred beats per minute. He developed severe abdominal pains that were diagnosed as irritable bowel syndrome. He developed insomnia that was diagnosed as night terrors and depression. I was really scared. Was all this caused by the drugs?

I tried to correspond with the prescribing physicians, but as of this writing I have received no replies. Fortunately, my ex-wife took Kevin to a new pediatrician who immediately took him off all these medications; thank goodness, all the symptoms cleared. These drugs scare me. What was most frustrating for me was knowing that neither diagnosis was even close to being accurate. Both boys maintain excellent grades. Kevin is skinny and, like most boys, doesn't have much padding on his bottom. Therefore, he squirms in his seat and sometimes even stands next to his desk while doing his work. That's all he ever did wrong as far as I could determine.

Boys are at a disadvantage when being evaluated for ADD or ADHD. They tend to have more difficulty sitting still. They are more robust than girls. Our society allows them more latitude than girls to play rougher and be more active. Settling down in school is more difficult for them. Furthermore, you may be surprised to read later in this chapter how these diagnoses are made. My child was put on drugs that were life threatening, based on a nebulous and incorrect diagnosis. This may be happening to you, so it's my hope that this chapter will help you avoid such a frightening situation as mine.

DEALING WITH ADD AND ADHD MYTHS

Obviously, this book is antimedication and differs drastically from the medical and psychological treatment practices that are currently popular. My intention is not to confront the medical, psychological, and educational communities but to win them over. My hope is that the Caregivers' Skills Program will lead to further research and improvements in drug-free treatment for children with attentional problems.

If parents are willing to say no to the use of these drugs when being pressured by the professional community, I think it best to understand some very important issues. The best way to do this is to arm people with an understanding of some of the myths about ADD and ADHD. So let's look at the seven most common myths.

Myth 1: ADD and ADHD Are Diseases

The diagnostic manual for psychiatry and psychology states that no laboratory tests can diagnose these disorders (American Psychiatric Association, 1994, p. 81). No findings have produced reliable evidence of a disease. Yet just about every form of treatment currently in vogue is aimed at treating a disease with chemicals—a disease no one can prove even exists.

There is no evidence that any bodily, brain, or nervous system malfunction causes these behaviors. As stated in the first chapter, a lot of scientists have been searching for this so-called disease for years, with no substantiated results. Fortunately, more and more professionals are beginning to believe that this is not a disease but a problem of poor thinking patterns and lack of motivation (Kendall, 1996; Breggin, 1998). I deeply believe that nothing medical causes children to not pay attention and to misbehave. They simply do not pay attention and they do misbehave.

One may ask, Why have these diagnoses exploded and become so prevalent in the last fifteen or so years? Depending on which literature you read, it's estimated that between two to four million children are diagnosed as ADD or ADHD, a growth of over 400 percent since 1988. Where did this mystery disease come from? Why did we not see so many children in previous generations with these patterns of behavior?

Consider that there are other psychiatric diagnoses of even more severe behavioral disorders. Examples are conduct disorders, where children break the law or become violent, or oppositional-defiant disorder, where children are openly defiant and rude to their parents. Few mental health professionals think of these last two conditions as diseases; they are seen as behavioral problems. What is this difference in viewpoint based on? Certainly no scientific or empirical rationale exists for the difference. Yet some persist in viewing attentional disorders as diseases and present this opinion as if it were irrefutable fact.

Let's consider this disease issue a little more closely. There are four categories of diseases: infectious, contagious, traumatic, and systemic. In infectious and contagious diseases a germ of some sort causes the diseases. We know ADD and ADHD cannot be that. Trauma diseases require an outside insult to the body, such as a blow to the head. We can rule that out. That leaves systemic diseases in which the cells or chemicals of the body begin to malfunction, such as with cancer.

Ah, you say—there's the culprit. Not so fast. If a systemic disease runs in families, that means it is genetic but cannot increase in the percentage of diagnosed cases in succeeding generations. A systemic disease remains fairly stable from one generation to the next or may increase only slightly. But it cannot increase between 400 and 500 percent in ten years, as has the occurrence of ADD and ADHD. Nongenetic systemic diseases also cannot increase unless there is a dramatic, toxic change in the environment, like massive radiation. So how can the attentional disorders be increasing at the reported rates? Someone has to explain where this massive disease epidemic is originating.

There are about ten different theories, which I cited earlier, each implicating a different problem with the brain, the nervous system, or the chemicals of the nervous system as *the* culprit causing this mysterious disease. Are all these theories correct, or are none of them correct? The scientists responsible for each theory claim that their theory and research are correct. Research by other scientists consistently fails to support the claims made by the original theorists.

What if one of these theories eventually turns out to show changes in the brain or nervous system? This still does not mean disease is present. The environment produces changes in the brain and nervous system, which Breggin (1998) points out in his book.

How we are raised, what stresses we face, and where we grow up—in the city or country—are registered in the brain by chemical and cellular changes. To define a disease it must be shown that these bodily and nervous system malfunctions come first and actually *cause* the ADD or ADHD behaviors. If the environment causes the behaviors and brain changes, the result is a disorder, not a disease. If we define the changes that result from the environment as diseases, then everything we do or say is a disease. That is absurd.

I believe that all bodily or brain changes that have ever been measured in ADD or ADHD children are the result of their environment and therefore are disorders and not diseases. Disorders can be treated behaviorally, without the need for medication.

Are you beginning to understand that so far there is no disease and that amphetamines are only a pretext disguised as a treatment for something that is not there? The amphetamines only camouflage the problem. Is it worth the risks to let the confused professionals bully you into putting these chemicals into your child's body when, after thirty years, researchers have failed to support their disease theories?

Even if well conducted research were to reveal physiological differences, it would still not mean the presence of a disease. Such differences could not only be the result of environment but also from long periods of being on Ritalin, or related drugs, or even the result of the constant, self-induced state of agitation ADHD children keep themselves in. If these differences were truly ever found, they'd have to be very subtle because we're having so much trouble finding them. And even then these differences would probably be within the normal range for kids that merely have more active levels of behavior and not a disease.

It is important to remember that if such differences were found it really doesn't matter as far as the content of this book is concerned; the methods you'll be learning work anyway. It would make for some interesting research should any physiological differences ever be found to see if they subside after successful behavioral intervention. Once the child is calmed down, would these hypothetical differences also calm down?

Myth 2: Psychological Tests Support the Diagnosis of ADD and ADHD as Diseases

No psychological test can indicate an ADD or ADHD disease. These tests are merely checklists, rating scales, or observations of a child's attention during the test administration. They are merely alternate ways of observing that the child is either not paying attention or is misbehaving. If the child gets enough points or check marks, he is arbitrarily labeled ADD or ADHD. If he gets a lower score, he does not get the label.

Save yourself hundreds of dollars. You can get an even better diagnosis by merely observing the child. Remember Kyle? Which was more accurate, the results of a test or his mother's observation that he could sit patiently for hours working on his rock collection? These tests are only structured guides for observing behavior. They do not measure abnormalities in the body or brain. They do not measure a disease. When a psychologist says your child tested positive for ADD or ADHD, we poor parents are deluded into a misperception that this is a disease. Do not confuse a psychologist's label with a disease. The tests only confirm the labels. They do not indicate or detect any disease entity.

Myth 3: But the Doctors Say My Child Has ADD or ADHD

Your child "has" nothing of the sort. The doctor has assigned a label that sounds like it names a disease. If I change the names of the diagnoses to *inattentive* and *highly misbehaving*—IA and HM—notice the change in the way you perceive the problem behaviors. Merely changing descriptions of problems can change the way we perceive them. Later in this book, I make a plea to the psychological and medical communities to make this labeling change. I believe it would reduce the considerable confusion surrounding these behaviors.

Linda Seligman (1995), an expert on psychiatric and psychological diagnoses, points out that modern diagnoses are moving away from pejorative-sounding labels. *Pejorative* means that the labels either sound negative or infer the presence of a disease underlying an abnormal behavior, even though no such disease exists. This is what I am suggesting be done with the ADD and ADHD labels. If the labels were IA and HM, parents and professionals could alter their perceptions from the idea of disease to one of normalcy.

Myth 4: Ritalin Has a Paradoxical Effect That Supports the Disease Notion

For those of you unfamiliar with the term *paradoxical effect*, it means that giving a child a stimulant drug such as Ritalin has the opposite effect from stimulation, that is, it causes them to slow down their behavior and pay better attention. It was believed that this paradoxical effect only occurred in ADHD children and therefore was proof that these children were different—that they had a disease.

Yes, Ritalin does slow down behavior, but it neither supports the disease idea nor confirms the diagnosis. Amphetamines produce the same effects for everyone: adults, normal people, people with conduct disorders, and people with oppositional-defiant or anxiety disorders. They affect healthy animals the same way. They have a calming, subduing effect. These drugs were popular in the 1950s and 1960s with college students; amphetamines helped them study for exams and pull all-nighters. They were even given to soldiers in combat in several wars to calm them down and help them stay alert. This paradoxical effect works for just about anyone.

Here's an interesting idea: Why not give these children cocaine? By golly, you might get even better results! I mean if we're going to load them down with drugs to control them, let's go all the way. Sound ridiculous? Well, Sigmund Freud used cocaine around the turn of the century to help him work late at night; it helped him stay alert and concentrate for long hours. He liked the drug so much that he wrote a scientific paper on it ("On Coca") praising its use. Later, when the negative consequences of the drug took over his life, he publicly reversed his position.

Myth 5: My Doctor Says Ritalin Is a Mild and Safe Drug

If I believed the chemicals prescribed for our children were perfectly safe, I would have no quarrel with medicating them. But our current level of research on these chemicals is primitive, and I don't want to risk our sons' and daughters' well-being. Do you remember any drugs that were supposed to be perfectly safe but were later proved harmful? How about Thalidomide? Or even Ex-Lax!

Yes, many articles state that Ritalin is a relatively mild amphetamine. However, please recall that in the Federal Government Control Act of 1988, Ritalin is classified in Schedule II, the same category as cocaine, opium, and morphine. This indicates that it has a high potential risk for abuse and addiction.

Short- and Long-Term Side Effects

In addition to the coverage in Chapter One of the dangers of addiction, we need to look at other serious problems. Do you think these drugs only go directly to the brain parts that control behavior? No. They go all over the body and can have effects for which they were neither designed nor intended.

These unintended side effects are divided into (1) short-term side effects, which occur either immediately or within several weeks after beginning the drug, or (2) long-term side effects, which may not appear for many years. Short-term side effects of amphetamines, including methylphenidate (Ritalin), in children include insomnia (which my son Kevin developed), tearfulness, rebound irritability, toxic psychosis, personality changes, nervousness, skin rash, fever, nausea, dizziness, headaches, heart palpitations, dyskinesia (strange tongue and face movement), drowsiness, blood-pressure changes, cardiac arrhythmia (which Kevin developed), angina (chest pain), and abdominal pains (which Kevin also developed).

Toxic psychosis (which means that the drug is at a poisonous level and the child is losing reality contact) can occur in rare instances. Anorexia and weight loss may occur. Complications such as depression, suicidal thoughts, or even Tourette's Syndrome (a neurological disorder characterized by tics and bizarre verbalizations) can occur unless the drug is carefully monitored. Scary, huh?

Of most concern to me are the effects that occur years later—the long-term side effects. Long-term studies are rarely conducted on drugs. (Bet you didn't know that.) Why? There are several reasons. First, studies that take years to conduct are extremely expensive. Who is going to pay? The answer is: just about no one. Second, researchers are usually professors. They want raises and promotions that are typically determined by publishing research findings in scientific journals. Do you think they want to wait ten or twenty years to publish? Therefore, they rarely embark on long-term research projects. And third, the pharmaceutical companies are not required to perform long-term research on their drugs. In addition, it is not in their interest to conduct long-term studies because adverse findings would have a negative impact on sales, and you know that is the last thing they want.

However, the results of a few medium-term studies have recently been published in the scientific journals, and they do not look favorable for Ritalin. One issue is the long-term side effect that Ritalin interferes with normal growth in children. This is called growth inhibition or growth suppression. Ritalin suppresses growth while a child is on it by interfering with growth hormones. We have no way of knowing how big or how tall a child would have become if he had never taken the drug (Weiner, 1982). A recent study seems to indicate that height and weight gain may indeed be somewhat impaired by these drugs (Rao and others, 1997). I have noticed that a number of teenagers referred to me who had been on Ritalin for several years were smaller than other teenagers of the same age.

Another study may indicate problems with the immune system (Auci, 1997). Please note the dates of these studies. Only recently are the data coming in on longer-term effects. Much more long-term research is needed.

Once again, parents, are you willing to accept these possible risks to control your child's behavior? Or is the course of treatment proposed in this book beginning to sound more and more inviting?

Drug Holidays

What about drug holidays? These are time periods such as evenings, weekends, and holidays from school during which your child does not take the drugs. Ask your doctor this: "If these drugs are so safe, why are drug holidays so necessary in the first place? And furthermore, why is it OK for my child to be controlled in school but not when he's with me?"

If you teach children drug taking, they will learn drug taking. I very much fear training children to use drugs in order to handle their emotional and behavioral problems. Drugs are useful when they are necessary and when they are restricted to the shortest term possible. To me, a good physician is one who is most reluctant to write a prescription for any type of chemicals.

Your child's doctor may have assured you that Ritalin is not addictive. Your doctor may truly believe that. But doctors tend to think of addiction as a physical condition; I am more concerned about the psychological addiction, which is much more powerful. Each textbook I use in my psychopharmacology course makes this same point. The euphoria, the sense of peace and calm, and the escape from stress, anxiety, and depression make these drugs extraordinarily and powerfully addicting—psychologically. Did you know that these drugs, especially Ritalin, are being sold on the streets for the express purpose of getting high?

Physicians are not as knowledgeable about medications as you might think or hope. Too many medications are on the market for physicians to remain current in every detail and research finding.

When I was supervising and teaching students in medical school, I learned that physicians generally have a limited arsenal of about forty or fifty drugs from which they typically prescribe. When morning rounds are conducted in a university medical setting, doctoral-level pharmacologists consult with the doctors. Most of pharmacists' training focuses exclusively on medications, and therefore they are more familiar with hundreds of drugs. Doctors have to study numerous other things like diagnosis of diseases, anatomy, physiology, and so forth, in addition to seeing patients all day. They can't keep up with it all.

I am suggesting that you not rely so readily on your doctor's opinion. You are a consumer and you have a right to question any drugs recommended for your child. If you wish, call a medical school and talk to a pharmacologist before beginning your child on a highly questionable medication. The ones I've talked to do not like Ritalin or any of the other amphetamines.

Myth 6: If ADD and ADHD Are Not Diseases, I Must Have a Lazy Child

Since the 1970s the composition of the American family has drastically changed. Two-parent families make up fewer than 50 percent of households; in 85 percent of these, both parents are working. The single-parent household makes up the other 50 percent. Extended families—grandmothers, grandfathers, aunts, uncles, and cousins— are rare because relatives often live in distant states.

All of this has had an impact on the way we parent children. With parents being stressed and rushed, the time for tender nurturance of children is drastically reduced. Child development studies indicate that children who are given little nurturance have trouble later in life with giving nurturance. They are also prone to depression, as psychiatrists Beck (1988) and Lewinsohn and Rosenbaum (1987) have pointed out. Most important, as Breggin (1998) suggests, they have trouble controlling their behavior and are often labeled ADHD.

In my research I have stressed the importance of values in the developing personalities of children. The careful and delicate molding of values such as loving to learn, being willing to work hard, developing long-range goals, and deferring gratification underlie children's motivation to take school seriously and to work hard. If we fail to instill these values, which takes years of patient teaching, I deeply believe we create children who do not wish to pay attention in class and do not care about controlling their behavior, that is, ADD-ADHD or IA-HM children.

Beck (1988) states that modern psychology and psychiatry are in the midst of a "cognitive revolution" (p. 1). What he means is that cognitive therapy is becoming the predominant form of therapy in practice. This form of therapy focuses on our thinking patterns and on our beliefs as determinants of the way we behave.

Cognitive therapy was introduced in the 1960s by Albert Ellis. In the 1970s this form of therapy merged with the well-researched and scientifically based techniques of behavior modification and formed what is now called cognitive-behavioral therapy—the focus of this book. We will not only be working to change your child's behavior but we will be changing his or her thinking patterns and belief systems.

This book offers solutions. It teaches you effective and rigorous parenting skills so you can stop the ADD or ADHD behavior and thinking patterns. However, this is not a quick fix. What I offer here requires you to parent your children actively. You must give the requisite time and attention for this system to work. And once you get the ADD or ADHD behavioral patterns under control, you still need to give your children time, attention, love, and guidance in order to retrain their thinking and beliefs. We can control their behaviors, but you must tenderly nurture them and patiently teach them the values they need in order to want to behave and to succeed in school. The true key to success is not merely getting children's behavior under control but reteaching them values.

So it is not accurate to say that ADD or ADHD children are lazy. They are confused. Their values are confused. We are failing our children by not being there for them. If they are to change, we must change. We must slow our lives down, decide the values we wish to teach them, and then patiently cultivate these values in our children.

Myth 7: The Teachers and School Systems Are at Fault for So Many ADD and ADHD Children

I need to divide the answer to this myth into four parts: (1) teachers, (2) curricula, (3) school discipline, and (4) class size.

Teachers

I have been an educator for thirty years at various levels: elementary school, intermediate school, college, graduate school, and medical school. I have practiced in and consulted for school systems under many circumstances, including inner-city, rural, and suburban schools. I can honestly say that I have rarely encountered a poor teacher. Most teachers I have met work extraordinarily hard and are devoted to their students.

Politicians find teachers a convenient and helpless target for the poor national test scores our children obtain—poor, that is, compared to other countries. But it is not the fault of our teachers. I have observed over the years that children who come from families that instill deep values, such as a love for learning, hard work, integrity, and achievement, do well in school, whereas children who come from families in which there is little time and nurturance devoted to the development of values do poorly. As a matter of fact, motivated children with strong values pay attention and work hard and do not wind up with ADD or ADHD labels. It is time we stopped blaming teachers.

Curricula

I believe that if educators and psychologists collectively search for the elements of curricula that can excite children, we will have fewer cases of ADD and ADHD. New, inventive, and creative approaches can be found. For example, I have conducted parenting workshops in high school and found teenagers to be eager and enthusiastic to learn these skills. Why not incorporate more hands-on activities with younger children?

I periodically take my sons to a nearby gem mine where they can dig for precious stones and use sluice boxes to separate the dirt from the stones. They love it. They can identify the variety of rocks and gems much faster and more accurately than I can. Why can't the traditional classroom activities be taken outside in such a fashion to make learning fun and exciting? When I taught elementary school in the inner city, I scheduled many adventurous educational class trips that I believed the children loved.

Content and presentation that can excite students are empirical issues that can be answered through more research. I deeply believe we can find these answers, especially for children who don't pay attention well.

Breggin (1998) says, "Children labeled ADHD do not differ from other children in what they need. If a child doesn't focus in class, it means that the child doesn't have a relationship to the teacher that fulfills the child's educational needs. Think about that: If the teacher were empowered to grab the child's imagination, the child would pay attention" (p. 252).

We need to find a combination of teaching methods and subject matter that gets young people excited about school. As Palmer (1998) points out in his book *The Courage to Teach*, we can connect with students by a combination of approaches, including being active in the community, using electronic media, leaving the classroom for outside activities, and finding other inventive ways to reach students. This is consistent with turn-of-the-century educator and philosopher John Dewey, who wrote that education should be part book learning and part experience.

Thus finding inventive ways to enrich both the curricula and pedagogical techniques will perhaps get more and more children to love school.

Discipline

Discipline is a sticky issue. I do not believe in corporal punishment by school officials. Unfortunately, schools have few effective methods they can use to discipline children who are disruptive in class—often the so-called ADHD children. In addition, the most frequent complaint I hear from teachers is that when children are disruptive, they often cannot get parents to cooperate and enforce discipline at home in order to get their children under control. What then can teachers do? The typical solution is a pill and a glass of water.

In this book I offer specific methods of discipline for parents to use in controlling a disruptive child when the teacher brings the problem to their attention. Parents should read this book and cooperate. I feel that if a highly disruptive child interferes with the learning environment for other children and his or her parents refuse to help get the situation under control, then the child should not be permitted to return to school until the parents do cooperate. Unfortunately, most laws will not permit this. The irony is that instead of meaningful discipline, we are willing to shove poisonous chemicals into our children's bodies.

Class Size

Studies show that smaller class size creates a more effective learning environment. A study by Finn, Achilles, Bain, and Folger (1990) found that smaller classes yield significant improvement in reading and math performance for inner-city and minority children. Smaller classes help with early school adjustment (Gullo and Burton, 1992). Russell Barkley, for many years, has advocated smaller classes for children with attentional problems.

However, other studies show that slightly larger class size is important to help the young develop social skills and peer relationships (Feld, 1991). In my work I have found that too small a class size fosters the cognitive dependency problem I discussed earlier.

The solution, I believe, lies in finding optimal class sizes—large enough to foster the development of social skills and independent cognitive abilities but small enough to provide sufficient individual attention. Classes should also be small enough to minimize distractions, such as excessive noise, and to allow teachers to control the behaviors of more rambunctious children.

My review of the research literature indicates that, to date, the prevailing opinion leans toward a class size of about fifteen to eighteen. Unfortunately, class size in many parts of this country exceeds thirty students, and sometimes forty. No teacher can maintain control of classes that large, and few children can get their academic needs met under these conditions.

WHAT IS THE CAREGIVERS' SKILLS PROGRAM?

In my practice and research I have pinpointed what is necessary in behaviorally treating children to alter specific behavioral patterns, restructure the thinking and motivational patterns, and eliminate completely the need for drugs for what is diagnosed as ADD or ADHD.

The Caregivers' Skills Program differs from other approaches and produces dramatic, positive changes in children by completely eliminating the ADD and ADHD patterns without the use of medication.

Difference 1: Stop the Drugs to Allow the Training of New Behaviors

The drugs do control the behaviors, but then they serve to mask the problem behaviors and thus block the way for effective change. The behaviors must be occurring if we are to change them. To begin the Caregivers' Skills Program, children must be taken off the drugs before their behavioral and thinking patterns can be changed. Please only do this under your doctor's directions.

Let me explain a little further. In order to train a child to attend to her behaviors and learn self-control, we must have her in the state or situation where the problem behaviors occur. If Nancy is a behavioral problem in class and the teacher puts her desk in the back of the room, away from the other children, then the problem behaviors will not occur and we cannot teach her to *learn* to be aware of her behaviors and control them. The same is true for Ritalin. It controls the behaviors and, as a result, Nancy loses opportunities to learn to control herself.

Difference 2: Treat Them as Normal and Capable Children

I believe that attentional disorders are not diseases but patterns of inappropriate behaviors, faulty thinking, and lack of motivation. I view so-called ADD and ADHD children as normal, but ones in whom the motivation to learn and perform well in school has failed to take hold and who have learned to behave in obnoxious ways. I also view them as lacking in strong, positive values.

Because neither ADD nor ADHD exists as a medical condition, I am changing the terminology for this book. I hope the new terms will catch on with the professional community. From now on the children will be referred to as inattentive (IA) and highly misbehaving (HM).

I believe that the solution to eliminating IA and HM patterns is to teach parents and professionals the requisite skills to produce the desired changes. This book teaches easy-to-understand, step-by-step parenting skills.

Difference 3: Change the Way They Think as Well as the Way They Behave

The focal point of the Caregivers' Skills Program is to understand that IA and HM children have the classic mental state or cognitive thought pattern of "not thinking." Once you understand this, everything in my method makes sense; you'll understand why it works so well and why other programs collapse. Ways of thinking are called cognitive patterns. I credit the concept of *not thinking* to my graduate school classmate and eminent psychologist Phil Kendall. My work focuses on how to change these faulty cognitive patterns.

Other traditional and typical approaches recommend a standard package of special tutoring, individual attention, medication, a few behavior modification ideas, and perhaps a token economy program at home and at school. These methods actually highly reinforce and perpetuate the not-thinking pattern, as I stated in Chapter One. Parents, teachers, and tutors constantly stay close to the child— prompting, guiding, cueing, coaxing, pointing things out, reminding, and warning. *The adults do all the thinking for the child, who becomes highly dependent on assistance from other people.* Adults become the child's reminder machines. The youngster does not learn the most basic, fundamental components necessary for obliterating the IA and HM (ADD and ADHD) patterns—namely, to focus, remember, pay attention, and monitor his own behavior. We don't want mere compliance to what the adult is requesting. We want the child to think and remember on his own.

By the way, pharmaceutical companies have yet to find a medication that teaches children how to think. Drugs help to focus and to reduce undesirable behaviors but not to learn how to think. Once the medications are taken away, not thinking still plagues the child and all the problems reemerge. A new trend is to continue the drugs into adolescence and adulthood, which heightens every risk we discussed earlier.

Difference 4: Change Your Parenting

Every topic in this book reverses much of what other approaches advocate. The Caregivers' Skills Program teaches children to think and monitor their behaviors at all times—*on their own*, with as little reminding and cueing as possible.

Whereas other books focus on school-performance problems of the IA or HM child, I believe that problematic behaviors and thinking patterns manifest themselves in both school and the home. School performance will never be fully controlled until the child learns to think and behave correctly at home. Actually, once the child is under control at home, improving school performance is relatively easy. In approximately 80 percent of my cases, once behavior is under control at home, schoolwork *automatically* improves without further intervention. (If school performance problems persist, Chapter Ten will show you some further steps for getting this problem under control.)

Difference 5: Change All Misbehaviors, Not Just the Behaviors of Impulsivity or Not Paying Attention

The Caregivers' Skills Program focuses on every behavioral and motivational problem, including aggression, that may occur both in the home and at school. I teach parents exactly what behaviors and thinking patterns are producing IA or HM problems and how to correct them. A comprehensive approach is the only way to eliminate troublesome patterns. We work on behaviors that precede IA and HM (ADD or ADHD) behaviors. We don't wait until they are out of control; we move in when there is even a hint of not thinking or not paying attention or not minding their behavior. Yes, this is a rigorous approach, but it is a lot safer and far more effective than drugs or patchwork behavioral approaches. The piecemeal approaches mentioned before are doomed to repeated collapses of any initial gains.

The Caregivers' Skills Program uses a form of discipline that is neither punitive nor reinforcing to undesirable behaviors. I teach the use of *time out* in a way that requires IA or HM children to think and remain alert at all times to what they are doing and what is going on around them. It is applied in a very rigorous fashion and in a very different way than you may have learned elsewhere.

Remember this: Once you begin working with your child, *you should see dramatic results within one to two weeks.*

3

THE IMPORTANCE OF EFFECTIVE PARENTING

I n this chapter we'll look at the forces in our society that are making it increasingly difficult to parent effectively and the damage that can result. We'll also look at why effective parenting is so crucial for the IA or HM (ADD or ADHD) child.

CONFESSION OF AN INATTENTIVE, BORED, AND UNMOTIVATED CHILD

When I was a kid, Richard Boone, star of television's "Medic" and "Have Gun Will Travel," saved my life. My grades were terrible and my standardized tests indicated that I was well below average in intelligence. Because my studies did not interest me, I was highly distractible and sometimes disruptive in class. Even today it's painful for me to recall the disdain and humiliating corporal punishment I received from my teachers.

Then at age ten I saw "Medic" and realized I wanted to be a doctor when I grew up. I had direction for the first time in my life. Suddenly my school lessons took on meaning and relevance. I became an excellent student, and the love of learning and positive feedback I received from my family and teachers raised my self-esteem. My grades soared and stayed high.

Had I been growing up in the nineties rather than the fifties, I probably would have been diagnosed as ADD or ADHD and placed on a mind-altering drug. In fact, I was simply inattentive, bored, and very unmotivated.

I have counseled many, many children whose attentional disorder miraculously disappears near the end of the school year when their teacher threatens to fail them and have them repeat the year if they don't start passing tests and doing their homework correctly. Many of them can suddenly do everything they supposedly could not do.

A similar example is a child who can sit in front of the television or play Nintendo for hours but can't concentrate on tasks she doesn't choose to do, usually schoolwork. Experts often rationalize this by saying that the brain chemistry of so-called ADD and ADHD children allows them to do well on tasks that produce immediate or rapid reinforcement—TV, Nintendo, or computers—but not on tasks in which reinforcement is delayed, prolonged, and postponed. Viewing this as a selective disease simply doesn't make sense. I can't think of any disease that could manifest itself with such refined selectivity. I see this as a motivational problem. The IA or HM child simply does what she likes and doesn't do what she doesn't like.

THE UNDERLYING LACK OF MOTIVATION

In reviewing my case folders of children referred to me with the diagnosis of ADD or ADHD over the last decade, I have very rarely had a failure in treatment using the behavioral methods in this book. There are two parts to the secret of this success rate. The first is *to use behavioral techniques correctly*, which is what this book is all about. The second is, after getting their behaviors under control, *to give children the time and attention they need in order to restructure and retrain their values so that school and achievement become important to them.* In the children I have seen who miraculously began performing at the end of the school year and who could play at their video games for hours, the underlying theme is the lack of motivation. Our task is to completely change that pattern by first getting their behavior under control, so we can get their full attention, so we can inspire their motivation. It's regrettable to view these children as having damaged brains and then to administer Ritalin or related drugs to them when they are simply children who are mischievous, unruly, and unmotivated.

POSSIBLE REASONS FOR OUR PREDICAMENT

For most parents, giving birth to a healthy baby is proof that miracles do happen. In two years, however, your joy can turn to frustration, anger, and even depression as your beautiful infant evolves into a full-fledged monster during the "terrible two's." The terrible two's can be many times worse than usual if you have a highly active and energetic child. If you have such a child and if you are confused and uncertain about how to parent him, you may actually be training him to misbehave and to be inattentive.

Stress on the Family

The majority of diagnoses in *Diagnostic and Statistical Manual of Mental Disorders* (4th edition)—I'll call it the *DSM-IV* from here on—are not considered diseases but maladaptions resulting from stress. This edition of the manual, which was published in 1994, is a text developed jointly by psychologists and psychiatrists that lists the symptoms or criteria that must be observed in order for any mental health professional to make a specific diagnosis. These criteria for diagnosis, however, do not include guidelines for designing treatment approaches. The *DSM-IV* criteria for attentional disorders are listed in Exhibit 3.1.

Exhibit 3.1. Diagnostic and Statistical Manual of Mental Disorders: Criteria for Attention-Deficit/Hyperactivity Disorder.

A. Either (1) or (2):

    (1) six (or more) of the following symptoms of *inattention* have persisted for at least 6 months to a degree that is maladaptive and inconsistent with developmental level:

Inattention

    (a) often fails to give close attention to details or makes careless mistakes in schoolwork, work, or other activities

    (b) often has difficulty sustaining attention in tasks or play activities

    (c) often does not seem to listen when spoken to directly

    (d) often does not follow through on instructions and fails to finish schoolwork, chores, or duties in the workplace (not due to oppositional behavior or failure to understand instructions)

    (e) often has difficulty organizing tasks and activities

    (f) often avoids, dislikes, or is reluctant to engage in tasks that require sustained mental effort (such as schoolwork or homework)

    (g) often loses things necessary for tasks or activities (e.g., toys, school assignments, pencils, books, or tools)

    (h) is often easily distracted by extraneous stimuli

    (i) is often forgetful in daily activities

    (2) six (or more) of the following symptoms of *hyperactivity-impulsivity* have persisted for at least 6 months to a degree that is maladaptive and inconsistent with developmental level:

Hyperactivity

    (a) often fidgets with hands or feet or squirms in seat

    (b) often leaves seat in classroom or in other situations in which remaining seated is expected

    (c) often runs about or climbs excessively in situations in which it is inappropriate (in adolescents or adults, may be limited to subjective feelings of restlessness)

    (d) often has difficulty playing or engaging in leisure activities quietly

    (e) is often "on the go" or often acts as if "driven by a motor"

    (f) often talks excessively

Impulsivity

    (g) often blurts out answers before questions have been completed

    (h) often has difficulty awaiting turn, often interrupts or intrudes on others (e.g., butts into conversations or games)

Reprinted with permission from the *Diagnostic and Statistical Manual of Mental Disorders* (fourth edition). Copyright 1994 American Psychiatric Association.

Attentional disorders in the *DSM-IV* are considered stress-related disorders. Therefore, let's look at the pattern of stresses experienced by children today so you can understand how lack of motivation, poor conduct, and inattentiveness can result. Let's begin by exploring the stresses a typical American family may be facing and how they can affect children.

Everyday Stresses

Consider the stress the normal two-parent family—perhaps your family—experiences today, and double this stress for the single parent.

The alarm sounds at six o'clock and you must rush to dress, put breakfast on the table, then make sure the little ones are ready for day care, the babysitter, or school. You may fight heavy traffic on your way to drop the children off or worry about leaving them alone and being responsible for locking the house, then getting to the bus stop, where they will stand unsupervised until the bus picks them up. Arrangements might also have to be made for the children when school is dismissed. Yours may be latchkey kids, returning to an empty house. They may be transported to day-care facilities, so you or your spouse must fight rush-hour traffic to pick them up on time.

By six o'clock, Mom and Dad face the mess left over from the morning's flurry of activity. Maybe your family plants itself in front of the television while eating dinner, communicating only minimally. Surveys indicate that this is now a typical pattern in the American home. Then within a few short hours, the kitchen must be cleaned, homework checked, and children bathed and tucked into bed.

At last you and your spouse can settle down, often too exhausted for conversation, let alone affection. Each of you, feeling (justifiably) overburdened, believes that the chores left undone must be the other's fault. Each of you may harbor anger and resentment toward the other for not assuming a fair share of household responsibility. Not very good for marital relations, is it?

Weekends are generally no better. No wonder tension within the family—your family—can run high. This tension within a home can be readily felt by children and can make them anxious and often rather hyper.

Author, theologian, and psychotherapist Thomas Moore, in his book *Care of the Soul* (1992), calls this harried and technologically based lifestyle the Modernist Syndrome. He states that psychological symptoms emerge from this type of lifestyle. Not only are adults affected by all this—so are children.

Note the reciprocal relationship between the tension and stress in the home and the IA or HM child's behaviors. The tension contributes to making the child agitated and hyper, which in turn adds to the parents' stress and tension, which further adds to the child's stress, and back and forth it goes. The result is a reciprocal, negative cycle.

Even worse, if you are a single parent the stress can be almost unbearable.

De Facto Neglect

Perhaps it is inevitable that some of your children's most basic needs are neglected. I'm not talking about food, shelter, clothing, and the like. Negligence in providing these necessities is called *de jure neglect,* which is the form of neglect that is often dealt with by the legal or justice system. I'm referring to emotional needs—love, nurturance, and time to interact meaningfully with the parent or parents. Although unintentional, such neglect can be devastating for your youngster's emotional development. This is called *de facto neglect,* which is neglect that is an unintentional and an unfortunate product of our harried lifestyles. It is the breeding ground for out-of-control, nonthinking, and unmotivated children.

Loss of Values

Even if you work to spend focused, nurturing, quality time with your children, half-hour sessions can do only so much to instill the values, goals, and ideals your children must learn through constant example and patient nurturance.

Moore (1992) suggests that a significant part of the solution lies in simplifying and slowing down our lifestyles. This is not a new idea. Philosophers such as Henry David Thoreau, psychoanalyst Carl Jung, and most eastern and western religions have espoused the importance of slower-paced and more simplified lifestyles. I offer some suggestions throughout the book that can perhaps help you move toward this goal.

Loss of the Extended Family

According to sociological research, an additional problem is the breakdown of the extended family—grandmothers, grandfathers, aunts, uncles, and cousins—as well as the fact that parents and children often no longer live near one another and are thus unavailable to offer support. The extended family structure gave powerful support to the values children learned and how they learned them. Children developed from all family members the motivation to work hard, to attend school, to take pride in doing a job well. Surrounded by family support and concern, they learned to focus on commonly held values and to stay on track.

Today, few children grow up surrounded by a large extended family. With family resources so diminished, parents often find themselves strapped to teach their children traditional values. No wonder we see fewer children who can focus on a task, work hard, stay on track, and succeed. Instead we see children who in recent years have been diagnosed with ADD or ADHD.

I believe increased daily stresses, unintended de facto neglect, tense family environments, and the loss of the extended family as a source of support and teaching, taken together, account for the massive increase in the diagnoses of ADD and ADHD. At the turn of the century, sociologist Emile Durkheim (1912) called this the Social Breakdown Syndrome. He pointed out that the breakdown of social values and support structures provides a breeding ground for the escalation of all types of human problems. I include the escalation of children's problems—not valuing their education and not being motivated to work hard.

Other childhood problems are also escalating. Since 1970 we have seen a 300 percent increase in delinquency, teenage suicides, drug and alcohol abuse, and senseless murders. All this is not happening in a vacuum. Our society has undergone major changes that are not necessarily good. All these indices require some major social reevaluating and readjusting. With this book we can begin learning healthy skills for parenting. We can begin making changes in the family.

Media

If attentional problems are indeed a product of the weakening of important values, perhaps the media are contributing to the problem. What are our children watching on television? Studies indicate that the average American child spends between five to seven hours each day watching TV. Are children watching shows that convey messages about the importance of family and education? Or are they watching shows about sex, violence, and crime? Listen to the words of their favorite music. When you pay careful attention, you may be surprised.

Media are powerful mechanisms for teaching, and what they teach are not necessarily the values we truly want our children to learn.

HOW GOOD PARENTING CAN REDUCE EVERYONE'S STRESS

The Caregivers' Skills Program (CSP) is a comprehensive parenting approach designed for IA and HM children that teaches you how to bring your child's behaviors under control. Knowing how to parent your child effectively eliminates his or her annoying and disruptive behaviors, which in turn reduces a lot of your stress. Your resulting calmness and the security of knowing healthy parenting skills serve to ease the tension in the home. This tense and strained environment underlies much of children's agitated behavioral patterns. Knowing how to parent your children will give them structure, that is, a knowledge of the boundaries and limits for their behavior. A much calmer household environment will result. We can disrupt the negative stress cycle and reverse it to a more positive cycle.

The model or outline for the CSP is shown in Figure 3.1. At the top are the caregivers who are trained in positive and negative control methods (reinforcement and discipline) to change the IA and HM child's behavior patterns (target behaviors). This model serves as the outline for this book. Everything we cover is specifically designed for changing the IA and HM child and keeping him away from Ritalin.

THE CAREGIVERS' SKILLS PROGRAM

The Caregivers' Skills Program is based on scientifically grounded principles of behavioral treatment methods and distilled into a clear and easily followed program for parents with IA or HM children. Everything in the CSP has been tried and tested over many years.

Figure 3.1. The Caregivers' Skills Program.

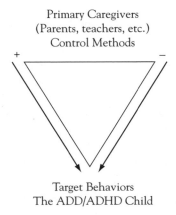

Primary Caregivers
(Parents, teachers, etc.)
Control Methods

+   −

Target Behaviors
The ADD/ADHD Child

The CSP puts a stop to negative interactions. The home environment becomes calmer, quieter, and more positive. The parents learn tools that are healthy and effective alternatives to yelling and hitting. Also stopped are the reminding, prompting, and cueing that contribute to children's cognitive dependency. Children must learn to think and be attentive at all times.

The CSP helps to eliminate the disruptive behaviors that consume so much of your child's time and energy and interfere with creativity. You will learn to reinforce your child's creative efforts—drawing, painting, writing—in ways that increase creative expressiveness. Most important, as your child settles down the two of you can be closer. You can begin the process of nurturing truly meaningful values that will guide him for the rest of his life.

As youngsters internalize proper values, they become more motivated and their ability to focus improves. Concentrating is a learned skill, which requires children to be enthusiastic and motivated.

Instinct Versus Knowledge

You may know people who seem to be naturals at raising well-behaved children, that is, they seem to have good parenting instincts. However, not all parents do. And some may never have learned the basic rules of good parenting. The purpose of this book is to teach the parenting skills needed to raise a well-behaved child, and especially to parent the IA or HM (ADD or ADHD) child. Using these principles, you should discover that parenting can be pretty easy—even a joy. Hundreds of parents have found that they were not as angry as they used to be, and they could stop feeling so guilty about their child's uncontrollable behavior and poor school performance because these things have disappeared.

Jonathan's Story

Jonathan was a cute, red-haired six-year-old. In school he spent more time out of his seat than in it. He frequently bothered other children and disrupted the class. He completed assignments only when he felt like it. Teachers called him "the monster." Other children made fun of him because of his tantrums. Sometimes he ended up brawling with one of his tormentors.

At home, Jonathan's uncontrollable behavior matched his school performance. His mother, a single parent, worked two jobs, and her parents cared for Jonathan after school. All of them added to his behavior problems by responding to him inconsistently. The grandparents gave in easily to his tirades and criticized his mother. Arguments between the grandparents and Jonathan's mother over their very different philosophies of parenting were a daily occurrence.

Jonathan cried frequently and told his mother that she did not love him—that no one loved him—and that he hated her. Being tense and on edge, Jonathan's mother reacted to him with constant threats, yelling, and spanking. Each year saw Jonathan getting progressively worse.

Several times his mother sought professional help. One therapist tried one-on-one therapy with Jonathan, which failed to produce results. Another put Jonathan on Ritalin and a token economy (behavior modification) program—a system of rewarding him with smiley-face stickers for good behaviors. None of this worked. A third therapist diagnosed Jonathan as depressed, then hospitalized him. The doctor prescribed antidepressants that made Jonathan lethargic. When his mother expressed her concern, the physician told her that the antidepressant needed more time to work. Week after week Jonathan became increasingly lethargic and weak. After a month his mother took him out of the hospital. Because she did so against the doctor's advice, her insurance coverage refused her claim. She declared bankruptcy because of the astronomical medical bills.

Jonathan's mother was referred to me by a former patient. I recognized that Jonathan had the typical behavior problems of the IA or HM child. I elected to do parent training, using the techniques covered in this book, and insisted that Jonathan's grandparents also participate. I saw all of them for five training sessions, then for follow-up appointments to refine their skills and answer questions.

Within three weeks of their training, Jonathan was a completely different little boy and a much happier child. His behavior improved dramatically at home and at school, all without medication of any sort. I have been in touch with Jonathan's mother periodically for several years. She reports that he has remained well behaved and happy. She also tells me that she is much calmer and feels much more confident as a parent.

Training the Adult, Not the Child

Focusing the training on primary caregivers fosters change more quickly and dramatically than when the therapist works with the child on a weekly basis using play or talk therapy. After twenty-five years of using the approach I advocate here, I have had hundreds of successful cases such as Jonathan's.

Of course a therapist must work directly with children if they are grieving a major loss or recovering from physical or emotional abuse. These youngsters have primary emotional problems and need to learn to cope with what they have suffered. But most of my patients are not emotionally disturbed; they exhibit behavioral problems.

How Emotional Problems Can Develop in the IA or HM Child

If the behavioral problems of IA and HM children are not brought under control, true emotional problems may develop. Tension and inconsistency in a household help create a breeding ground for the child to develop anxiety symptoms. In addition, the highly misbehaving child engenders negative reactions from just about everyone. Let's face it, these children are obnoxious. Teachers don't like them and frequently show it with looks of disdain or even disgust, which I painfully recall from my childhood. Teachers get mad at them and punish them frequently. These children fail tests frequently, and each failed test only reinforces their ever-lowering self-image. Other kids don't like them. They frequently get teased, taunted, and picked on. They are excluded from playing with the other children. Sometimes out of frustration they explode and get into physical altercations. Add all this to the negative treatment they receive from their parents, and year by year their self-image goes lower and lower, underlying their increasing emotional problems.

When caregivers learn how to parent more effectively and the environment becomes less stressful, children's emotional stability will improve. As their behaviors improve, the responses from teachers and other children will also improve, which will in turn enhance self-esteem. Having the child learn correct behavior is the best thing we can do for that child. A pill does not teach correct behavior.

WHY ALL CAREGIVERS MUST LEARN THESE SKILLS

Usually, parents and teachers have the most contact with the child, but others such as grandparents, older siblings, friends of the family, and day-care workers may play a major role in the child's development. I believe that everyone who spends significant time with the child must be included in the training to reduce family strife and to lessen the child's confusion. Remember that I included Jonathan's grandparents in the training. I train the teachers in these skills here at a college in Virginia. Training everyone who cares for a child provides consistency and continuity of care. Commonality of techniques reduces children's confusion. They quickly learn what is expected and proper behavior in any and all circumstances. In addition, the frequent arguing among caregivers subsides, further reducing household tension.

The techniques in this book are powerful. To be effective they require the adult to be firm, loving, and in charge. All children—particularly IA and HM children—need structure, guidance, and consistency. Failure to provide these essentials in a resolute manner can create a thoroughly confused child whose behavior is abominable.

4

BEGINNING THE CAREGIVERS' SKILLS PROGRAM

In this chapter we'll learn to identify the specific behaviors, called target behaviors, that we must focus on in order to help our children behave. We will compare our CSP list with the symptoms typically listed as problematic by the *DSM-IV*.

The shifting of focus from the *DSM-IV* symptoms to the CSP list of behaviors is a major innovation of this book. In this chapter we will review the basic reasons this shift is essential for working successfully with IA or HM children. We'll also carefully review the CSP target behaviors so that by the end of this chapter you'll have a firm grasp on which behaviors you can help your child change. Once target behaviors are eliminated, the IA or HM diagnosis can be resolved and all pressures to put your child on Ritalin will disappear.

UNDERSTANDING TARGET BEHAVIORS

The first task of changing the IA or HM child is to know clearly what behaviors need to be brought under control. These are behaviors that are readily observable, that is, they can be seen or heard.

For example, calling the child immature or disruptive or referring to emotional problems—or even diagnosing a child as having an attentional disorder—does not go far enough. We have to identify a child's observable behaviors that we wish to change—specific behaviors we can see or hear.

For example, if we refer to Johnny as immature, do we mean that he cries easily? Or speaks in a babyish voice? Or cannot pay attention and stay on task when doing his homework? Or loses his temper easily and hits other children? What if we say that Sally has emotional problems? Do we mean that she has temper tantrums? Or that she does not play well with other children? Or that she whines and pouts? To define Johnny's immaturity or Sally's emotional problems, we must look for specific, observable behaviors.

A basic rule in behavioral psychology is to reinterpret vague terms such as *immature* and *emotional problems* as observable behaviors. When we have simple, precise, clear behaviors that we can observe, we know exactly what to modify. The terms *immature* and *emotional problems* are commonly used by teachers and even psychologists, so be careful when you hear them. I mention them here for two reasons: (1) parents hear them frequently and (2) they often elicit a feeling of fear and panic in parents that something is terribly wrong with their child. Redefining these terms as observable behaviors is usually reassuring to parents because they can then see clearly what they are going to work on, that is, what their goals and objectives are.

IDENTIFYING TARGET BEHAVIORS

A target behavior is *habitual, frequently occurring, inappropriate*, and *distinctly observable*. We can see or hear it. All children occasionally act out many of the behaviors I'll describe. These are not problem or target behaviors unless they occur regularly and frequently. You need to use good judgment and fairness to determine what is normal and what is excessive.

The list of target behaviors you will be learning about here is very different from those listed in the *DSM-IV* (see Exhibit 3.1). Here are the differences between the two lists:

1. *Most of the* DSM-IV *behaviors occur in school.* Examples are fidgeting, pushing in line, and not paying attention. The CSP behaviors occur in both the home and school but are not included in the *DSM-IV* list. Examples include not doing as told, being defiant, using poor-me statements, and making negative verbal statements. Teachers cannot devote the time and attention needed to retrain an individual child in a large class. Parents can work on this retraining at home.

2. *In the CSP we focus primarily on behaviors at home instead of at school.* That reestablishes the parents as the child's authority figures. The emphasis of the CSP is on the parents because they carry out the consequences. This doesn't undermine the teacher's authority, however, because the teacher can easily notify the parents of any misconduct, and the consequences will be enforced at home.

3. *The behaviors listed in the* DSM-IV *occur late in the sequence of misbehaviors.* Examples are when the child has lost control—leaving her seat, running, pushing, blurting out answers. In the CSP list, many of the target behaviors occur earlier in the sequence of behaviors, at the preliminary stage and during milder forms of misbehaviors. For example, in the CSP we work on children complying immediately with a command to sit still and do their work. At a hint of being off task, consequences are enforced. We don't wait until children fidget or get up and walk around the room—behaviors defined in the *DSM-IV*.

A major difference between CSP and all other programs is the rigorous emphasis on controlling mere hints of misbehavior, way before the child loses control. In this way, the child learns that forgetting to monitor and control his behaviors early in the sequence will engender consequences. Therefore, the child has to learn to be more alert and vigilant to even the subtlest misconduct. A whine or a pout is dealt with in the CSP before the tantrum erupts.

4. *Some of the* DSM-IV *behaviors are vague.* For example, "failing to give close attention to details" or "failing to sustain attention" isn't clearly specific and observable. In the CSP we break this down to three easily observable components:

1. Looking: Are their eyes on their work or the speaker?

2. Listening: Can they answer the question, What did I just say?

3. Remembering: Can they answer the question, What should you be doing?

These three elements are the specific components of attentional problems that can be observed and altered by imposing consequences.

5. *Getting IA or HM children under control at home results in 80 percent of the children automatically improving in school.* Recall that the CSP predominantly emphasizes getting children under control at home. The *DSM-IV* list focuses predominantly on school. In the remaining 20 percent of the cases we will focus more on the *DSM-IV* list of behaviors occurring in school, but we'll learn how to coordinate efforts between the teacher and the parents. The parents, having firmly established their authority, will enforce the consequences at home, as indicated in systematic communication with the teacher, that is, in a daily report card (see Chapter Ten.)

Identifying Target Behaviors for the CSP

The list to follow is divided into four basic groups, including the seventeen target behaviors of the CSP that are common among IA and HM and other challenging children:

Group I: Active Manipulations

1. Not doing as told—noncompliance

2. Defying commands—oppositionalism

3. Temper tantrums

Group II: Verbal Manipulations

    4. Poor-me statements

    5. Negative statements

    6. Nagging

    7. Interrupting

    8. Physical complaints (saying they are ill or hurt when in fact they are not)

Group III: Inattention Behaviors

    9. Not paying attention

   10. Helplessness and dependency

   11. Dawdling

   12. Poor reading skills

   13. Poor school performance

Group IV: Other Common Misbehaviors

   14. Tattling

   15. Fighting with siblings

   16. Aggression

   17. Lying

Disruptive behaviors may apply much more often to HM children than to purely IA children, who often behave well but simply do not pay attention.

In order to succeed with your child, you must identify *each and every target behavior*, no matter what the child's official diagnosis. A key feature of the CSP is the comprehensive control of all target behaviors. Controlling only a few behaviors while allowing others to occur establishes a confusing learning environment and prevents the child from clearly comprehending what is expected.

A CHECKLIST FOR YOUR CHILD'S TARGET BEHAVIORS

I suggest you check the box before each target behavior that applies to your child.

Group I: Active Manipulations

In these three target behaviors you will notice the child escalating his defiance toward his parents in order to get his way.

☐ 1. Not Doing as Told—Noncompliance
      IA: very common; HM: very common

When your child is told to do something, he may fail to respond for different reasons. The child may choose to ignore your request, may not have learned to pay attention when being addressed, or may be an expert at tuning out. You may end up repeating the request more loudly, eventually yelling and threatening. Finally, when he is "ready"—and you are thoroughly exasperated—the child may finally comply. Does this sound familiar?

Our goal will be to get your child to respond immediately following your calm and firm request. Does this seem strict? Good. I don't believe children develop psychological scars by complying with a reasonable request. In fact, I *encourage* parents to be strict—although not punitive. *Strict* sets guidelines and boundaries; *punitive* hurts. I have found that once guidelines of "fair" expectations are drawn, children seem much more content.

If your child responds appropriately in some other way, such as by asking, "Mommy, may I first finish what I'm doing?" then you should react reasonably. For example, if you say no, you should have a good reason. Children need to learn good assertive communication skills, which can develop only if parents treat their assertive requests fairly. But if the answer is still no with a good reason, then the child should comply immediately with the request.

Doing as told (compliance) is a very important target behavior in the CSP for IA or HM children. I stated that we focus on behaviors that occur early, and long before the child loses control. If we rigorously and successfully focus on this behavior, notice that very few of the more out-of-control behaviors will ever occur.

Goal: Immediate response to requests or commands, with very few lapses.

❏ 2. Defying Commands—Oppositionalism
    IA: rare; HM: very common

HM (ADHD) children's response to commands often is overt defiance. A child may talk back, saying, "No, I won't" or may do the opposite of what you asked—for example, deliberately throwing down a toy when told to pick it up. The child may take on a sarcastic tone of voice or fold her arms across her chest as if to say, "No, I'm not going to, and you can't make me!" Defiance needs to be dealt with immediately. I'll explain how to do so in later chapters.

Defying commands also is a behavior that occurs early in the sequence of misbehaviors. If we focus on this behavior, more severe behaviors, such as the next one—temper tantrums—will be prevented from occurring.

Goal: No defiant behavior. None!

❏ 3. Temper Tantrums
    IA: rare; HM: very common

In my experience temper tantrums are the target behavior most frequently reported by parents of problem children. Many parents tell me that their child is a darling until they say no to the child's request. Then the battle ensues, often with parents finally giving in. Unfortunately, the parents' surrender actually reinforces the tantrums. The child learns to scream, slam doors, and fall on the floor in a rage in order to get his or her way.

Tantrums do not usually decrease as a child gets older; in fact, they typically get worse and may even carry over into adulthood. Practiced over many years, they become a deeply ingrained habit that can destroy many relationships. When I counsel married couples, temper tantrums are reported frequently as a problematic behavior. In almost every case, such tantrums began in childhood.

Some critics say that children should be taught to express their feelings, and I agree. The issue is how the feelings are expressed. We can teach offspring to express feelings assertively, such as "Mother, I'm angry at you because you aren't listening!" Expressing feelings through temper tantrums, however, should not be allowed.

Other critics view tantrums as necessary for ventilating anger that builds up in the child. Research shows that every violent outburst leads to an even more violent outburst, and allowing frequent expressions of violent temper actually makes the behavior worse over time. An occasional tantrum is normal, even for adults. But if tantrums occur more than a few times a year, then the behavior should be targeted.

Goal: No more than four or five temper tantrums a year.

Group II: Verbal Manipulations

The target behaviors in this group involve common verbal patterns that the child uses to get his way. Ask yourself if they work when used on you.

❑ 4. Poor-Me Statements
    IA: very common; HM: very common

Poor me's are self-deprecating statements or personal put-downs. Examples are:

No one loves me.

You love my sister more than me.

I'm stupid.

I can't do anything right.

Sometimes these statements are more humorous exaggerations:

You love the dog more than me.

Everyone has a better life than I do.

More serious statements include:

I want to die.

I'm going to kill myself.

Although such drastic statements as "I want to die" and "I'm going to kill myself" are most often manipulative, to be on the safe side, parents must always seek immediate professional help for children who use them often. A professional can best assess whether such threats should be taken seriously.

Also included in the poor-me's are such behaviors as pouting (hanging-lip syndrome), whining (puppy-dog syndrome), and crying (manipulatively, to get attention or to get his or her way).

Crying due to physical pain, exhaustion, or serious stress, which should only happen occasionally, is not a targeted behavior. Sometimes crying serves as a release for tension, but even this should only occur occasionally. Often when parents say a child is sensitive, I find a child who is an expert at making poor-me statements and who cries to manipulate.

Psychiatrist Thomas Harris, author of the best-seller *I'm OK— You're OK* (1969), notes that people who view themselves negatively and believe they're not OK behave in ways that perpetuate the feeling. Developing such an attitude can lead to a lifelong battle with depression. Children who get in the habit of repeating not-OK statements about themselves (the poor-me's) can start to believe them, resulting in a negative self-image. Verbal rehearsal can lead to *internalizing*—a psychological term that means they begin to believe what they have been saying. I think such statements are firmly internalized by age ten. Curbing such statements *before* they become internalized beliefs is of utmost importance. In the following chapters you'll learn exactly how to curb these verbal patterns.

If a child makes poor-me statements only rarely, you can comfort or console the child appropriately. But if poor-me's are frequent, nurturing will reinforce them and increase their frequency.

Note: If a child who has not previously expressed poor-me state-ments suddenly begins to show this behavior, attempt to learn if something specific may be troubling the child—perhaps a problem at school—and then try to remove it. The behavior will probably stop.

Goal: Very few expressions of poor-me statements. More than once or twice a month is excessive and requires work.

☐ 5. Negative Statements
   IA: common; HM: very common

Negative statements are the flip side of poor-me statements. Rather than personal put-downs, they criticize other people or sit-uations, suggesting the attitude that "You're not OK." Examples are:

Johnny's a creep.

I hate doing this.

Why do we always have to do this?

Do we have to go there?

He's stupid.

I hate you!

Some humorous ones:

I hope you go bankrupt.

I hate boys—they should be on another planet.

You never buy me anything.

The sooner you can identify and correct these statements—preferably in early childhood—the better the personality develop-ment of the child. Youngsters who internalize these beliefs by age ten learn to see the outer world as negative. They can become cyn-ical, critical, angry, and hostile. Trying to alter this attitude by ado-lescence becomes particularly difficult.

Goal: Only very few expressions of negative statements.

❑ 6. Nagging
     IA: rare; HM: very common

A child's nagging or repeatedly asking for something after he or she has been told no proves particularly annoying to many parents. When you tell your child no, explain why you are saying no. If your reasonable answer is still no and the child continues to nag, discipline should follow immediately but only the method of discipline covered later in the book. Be patient.
    Goal: No nagging.

❑ 7. Interrupting
     IA: rare; HM: very common

The child who constantly interrupts when you are talking to others can be as annoying as the child who nags. In extreme cases a child may even interrupt when you are on the telephone, possibly by picking up an extension to demand something from you immediately. Interruptions should be allowed only to report a dangerous or aggressive situation.
    Goal: No interruptions.

❑ 8. Physical Complaints
     IA: fairly common; HM: fairly common

When a child frequently complains of vague pains or of generally not feeling well but you have no indication of an actual medical disorder, the result can be that you won't believe your child when something is really wrong. As with poor me's and negative statements, a child can come to believe (internalize) his physical complaint and turn into a lifelong hypochondriac.
    Physical complaints most often occur when a child wishes to avoid a normal but stressful situation, such as a spelling test at school. Sometimes a truly stressful situation may underlie the

complaint—an overly critical teacher, for example, or a bully. In such cases if you can eliminate the problems, the complaints will disappear.

In the absence of excessive stress or any real physical malady, treat frequent physical complaints as manipulative and an inappropriate target behavior.

Unless your child exhibits symptoms of a real illness, send him or her to school. You can always ask a teacher or school nurse to contact you if the symptoms get worse. If you are uncertain, consult your family physician.

Goal: No physical complaints unless the child is truly ill or feeling pain.

Group III: Inattention Behaviors

All these target behaviors connect in a pattern of the child's "not thinking." Remember, this is the cognitive pattern of IA or HM (ADD or ADHD) children. You'll notice how each behavior is connected to the others, which means that each of these behaviors contributes to the overall pattern of inattention.

❏ 9. Not Paying Attention
    IA: very common; HM: very common

For many parents, the central problem of the IA or HM child is his inability to pay attention and remember things. As you probably realize, talking to such a child can be an exercise in futility. Children with attention problems are experts at tuning out. But just as being able to pay attention is a learned behavior, so is inattentiveness.

Attention has three parts: looking, listening, and remembering. Our first concern is *visual attention*, which you can observe easily. The child's eyes should focus directly on a task or directly on the adult speaking. Teachers call this "staying on task."

Goal: Set a strict goal for visual-task attention; eyes should divert only very briefly.

Focus next on *auditory attention*, which you cannot observe directly. To check whether the child is listening, you must ask, "What did I just say?"

Goal: If the child consistently cannot answer correctly, then listening should be treated as a target behavior; the goal should be to answer correctly every time.

Last, consider *remembering* or, conversely, *not forgetting*, which is a crucial behavior to develop in youngsters with attention problems. Most such children have been trained *not* to remember what they are told to do because parents repeat commands, nag, prompt, coach, or issue warnings. These are the techniques promulgated by other behavioral approaches; they defeat the goals of the CSP. The child has little incentive to use his own mind. If your child constantly tells you, "I forgot," when you ask, "Why haven't you done this?"—or when you ask your child who is not on task, "What are you supposed to be doing?" and his response is a completely bewildered look—then treat forgetting as a target behavior that will have negative consequences. Your child can learn to remember. It is a learned skill just like any other target behavior.

Goal: Allow no forgetting.

Overall Goal for Attention: The ability to keep eyes on work, to listen attentively, and to remember what has been said, with very few lapses.

☐ 10. Helplessness and Dependency
       IA: very common; HM: very common

Three forms of dependency overlap considerably.

1. *Task dependency* involves a child needing excessive support and prompting in order to begin or complete a task. With the IA or HM child, the task that readily comes to mind is homework.

2. *Cognitive dependency* involves not thinking throughout the day. The child does not pay attention to how to behave correctly in different environments, such as a restaurant, a grocery store, or the classroom. He doesn't monitor his own behavior throughout the day.

3. *Emotional dependency* is an irrational belief that one cannot be alone. The emotionally dependent individual experiences strong feelings of anxiety (fear) when alone. Emotional dependency also involves a second belief that an individual must always have someone taking care of him.

The IA or HM child's hallmark is the first two forms of dependency: task dependency and cognitive dependency. Currently popular behavioral treatments highly reinforce both patterns. Sitting with the child during homework and constantly prompting and guiding her work helps to get the task done but reinforces the child's task dependency. When you sit with your child, she doesn't learn to concentrate on her own and actively figure out how to complete the task. Focusing and concentrating on a difficult task requires considerable energy and resolute motivation.

Research also shows that IA or HM children have difficulty organizing their work without help; when they do the work, it's done in a hasty and sloppy fashion. Here, too, popular methods involve helping children organize and coaching them to work neatly.

In the CSP I've found that IA or HM children can do the work, can organize their materials, and can work neatly without constant coaching. You can show them one or two times how to organize but do not continue to prompt and coach thereafter. Let the consequences, which we'll soon learn, do the work. They'll then learn quickly.

In the CSP program once all target behaviors are well controlled, about 80 percent of the children automatically begin performing school-related tasks, such as homework and class assignments, quite well. This leads me to believe that often these children do know how to organize their work and do not really have skill deficits. Often their grades and the quality of their work improve to a passing grade level without teaching them organizational skills or constantly coaching them to work neatly. For the remaining 20 percent, a school program can be designed to enforce meaningful consequences as an external way to help motivate these children. In most cases it succeeds. A full chapter is devoted to this later.

Coaching and reminding throughout the day before entering new environments is also suggested in other approaches. This reinforces cognitive dependency. Some research indicates that IA and HM children lack the requisite social skills. Again this coaching reinforces the "not thinking" and the "not remembering" of these children. In the CSP when the coaching is eliminated and instead consequences are enforced, these children dramatically change in less than two weeks, demonstrating that they knew exactly how to behave, that they could control themselves, and that they do know the proper social skills.

Research on whether the constant coaching espoused by other approaches ultimately contributes to developing emotional dependency is lacking. However, because the CSP minimizes coaching and mobilizes independent functioning, it's safe to say that the program doesn't encourage the development of emotional dependency. In addition, in the CSP it is recommended that parents not do everything for the IA or HM child but instead should teach him skill building: teach and require him to perform self-help skills, including making his own bed, cooking, doing laundry, and so on. How to accomplish this is discussed in the next chapter. Sharing in household responsibilities helps children feel good about themselves, gain confidence, and feel like an integral and important family member.

(Notice that verbal manipulations such as poor me's, negative statements, and physical complaints occur very frequently with each form of dependence. Work on all these target behaviors simultaneously.)

Goal: The ability to work independently and assume responsibility. *Very rarely coach, remind, prompt, help, or warn the IA or HM child.* Enforce the consequences, using discipline methods described later, without warning.

☐ 11. Dawdling
         IA: common; HM: common

The child who begins tasks slowly and takes more time than necessary to complete them is a deliberate dawdler. Frequently, for example, the dawdler isn't ready on time for the school bus. Parents then wind up rewarding the child by driving her to school. Dawdling when doing homework is very common with both IA and HM children. By sitting and helping them, you are actually reinforcing the dawdling. I will recommend later in the book an effective way to deal with this problem.

Goal: Only very rare instances of dawdling—and never on school mornings.

☐ 12. Poor Reading Skills
         IA: very common; HM: very common

Attentional disorders and poor reading often go hand in hand. Many children diagnosed with IA or HM have been diagnosed with dyslexia, which means they have impaired reading ability. The reasons underlying reading problems are enormous and complex, and I won't attempt covering them in this book. Treatment usually involves relearning the fundamental reading skills taught earlier in school and approaching them slowly.

To help improve your child's reading skills I'll offer ten helpful hints to make reading enjoyable for your child in the chapter dealing with school-related problems.

❑ 13. Poor School Performance
        IA: very common; HM: very common

IA and HM children are of normal intelligence but consistently receive D's and F's in most academic subjects. Often these children are held back at least once in school, and their academic problems are the primary reason they are referred to psychologists. As I've noted, not paying attention has a lot to do with the poor academic performance of IA and HM youngsters.

To repeat my earlier statement: In 80 percent of my cases, when the home behaviors are completely under control, school performance automatically improves. If school performance does not improve, teachers will need to deal with the following target behaviors:

Academic Performance (IA and HM students)
    1. Not staying on task (or not paying attention)
        a. not looking at the work or the teacher
        b. not listening to instructions
        c. not remembering what to do
    2. Not finishing work on time
    3. Not doing work neatly
    4. Not doing work correctly and accurately and thus consistently getting grades lower than C (or a similar standard depending on the school's grading system)

Conduct (HM students only)
    1. Failing to be quiet
    2. Not staying in seat
    3. Blurting out questions without politely raising a hand
    4. Pushing in line rather than waiting and walking in line

Chapter Ten is devoted exclusively to analyzing and treating problems with school performance should it remain a problem after completely improving at home.

Goal: No grades below a C and no poor conduct grades. Many IA and HM children can begin to earn A's and B's.

Group IV: Other Common Misbehaviors

These target behaviors also apply frequently to youngsters with attentional problems, especially those in the highly misbehaving category.

☐ 14. Tattling
        IA: fairly rare; HM: fairly common

All children tattle occasionally. When tattling occurs frequently, treat it as a target behavior. In most cases I recommend that you tell the tattler to work things out with the other child. Working things out means being assertive and using good communication skills. Earlier we discussed inappropriate verbal behaviors—the poor me's, negative statements, and temper tantrums. When we discussed these verbal patterns, I mentioned the importance of teaching your child appropriate communication and assertion skills. Recall our discussion about how to substitute angry outbursts with assertive expressions of feelings. Don't try to teach the skills at the moment a target behavior occurs, because that inadvertently reinforces or conditions the behavior. If you talk with your child at the moment she is tattling, she becomes conditioned to getting attention and nurturing by tattling. You'll later learn how to discipline the tattler to avoid inadvertently reinforcing this verbal pattern.

It is best to try not to interfere, whether the problem involves playmates or siblings. Children develop social skills by trial and error, and developing appropriate social skills requires particular effort from IA and HM children.

Tattling is allowed, of course, if the child being tattled on is doing something dangerous or has become physically aggressive. In such cases tell the tattler she used good judgment in coming to you.

Goal: A minimum of tattling.

☐ 15. Fighting with Siblings
        IA: fairly common; HM: very common

Sibling fights create problems for many families. All siblings
sometimes get on one another's nerves and bicker or argue among
themselves. The behaviors of HM children can seriously annoy siblings; getting these behaviors under control often automatically
improves sibling relationships. (One note: parents should never
tolerate physical aggression of any kind and should always deal with
it strongly, as I advise in my discussion of aggression as a target
behavior.)

In dealing with sibling fights, avoid asking, "What's going on
here?" Once each child has related his side of the story, you will
have little idea who actually did what to whom. Instead, discipline
both parties immediately without asking questions. Of course if you
have observed directly who initiated the conflict or if you recognize
a pattern of disruptive behavior from one child rather than the
other, you may discipline that child only. Keep in mind, though,
that a child who looks like an angel may still be guilty of secret
taunting and teasing.

I advise parents to allow children to work out their differences
themselves. I have observed my ten- and twelve-year-old sons arguing with each other one minute and the next minute telling each
other "I love you."

One useful technique for cutting down on sibling fights is to
allow children to enter one another's bedrooms only with permission (assuming children have their own rooms). Then a child who
wishes to avoid a fight can quickly retreat to his or her room. This
privilege can be abused, however. I had two young girls as patients
who fought constantly. One evening the older girl's cat ran into her
sister's room. When the older girl knocked on her sister's door to
retrieve the cat, the younger girl was brushing her teeth. She continued to brush for over half an hour before saying no. The younger
girl lost room privacy privileges for a month.

Goal: No more than three or four loud, disturbing fights a year. However, allow mild squabbles and let siblings iron out their differences.

❑ 16. Aggression
    IA: rare; HM: occasionally

Aggression—violent contact with others, whether directly or using objects as weapons—is a low-frequency, high-priority behavior. Not many children exhibit aggressive behavior, but immediate action must be taken with those who do. A specific diagnosis of this disorder is defined for HM (ADHD) with aggression, and I devote a separate section of this book to the control of aggressive behavior.
    Goal: No aggressive behavior except when absolutely necessary for self-defense.

❑ 17. Lying
    IA: fairly common; HM: fairly common

A child may lie to avoid punishment or to gain something she probably would not get by telling the truth. Like aggression, lying is a low-frequency, high-priority behavior and should be dealt with at the earliest age possible. Children who lie early on become extremely skillful liars as they get older, and their lies become increasingly difficult to detect.
    Many parents ask me about imaginary play or fantasy, which is perfectly normal and should be permitted. Of course, imaginary play should decrease considerably as the child approaches the age of ten.
    Goal: No lying.

SUDDEN CHANGES IN BEHAVIOR

Before beginning to work on the behavioral problems it is a good idea to rule out other potential problems. A sudden surge in behavior problems can result from outside forces: a school bully picking on a child, a punitive teacher making a child nervous, the loss of a loved one, or marital conflict. When these situations underlie a child's misbehavior, parents might best try to remove the source. If the stress is severe, for example, suffering physical or sexual abuse or losing a loved one, professional help is strongly recommended. We are not dealing with a long-standing behavioral pattern, like target behaviors. Instead we are dealing with an emotionally upset child, with the upset resulting from a dramatic upsurge of stress. In the IA or HM child the behaviors get worse more gradually over a longer time period.

One child I tested turned out to have a rather low level of intelligence. His behavior problems resulted from his inability to learn at the same rate as the other children. He was placed in a slow learner's class and henceforth did well.

I have found, though, that lack of parenting skills is the primary reason for children's misbehavior, especially for the behavior problems of the IA or HM child.

A REVIEW OF THE TARGET BEHAVIORS

Take a few minutes to list the behaviors you have targeted for your child. If the list seems a bit overwhelming, take heart. In the chapters that follow, we'll be looking at some foolproof ways of dealing with these behaviors.

5

IMPROVING BEHAVIORS

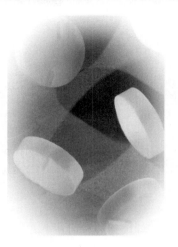

In this chapter we will learn to understand reinforcement as the means for improving desirable behaviors. We will review the differences between social and material types of reinforcers and the principles for applying them.

REINFORCEMENT VERSUS DISCIPLINE

Parents typically want to focus at first on discipline. During my first few years of teaching, I gave in to their wishes and taught discipline early, but I noticed we were not getting good results. Then I changed the order of the curriculum and began with how to reinforce—reward—children's correct behavior. Sure enough, there was a dramatic increase in the number of successful cases.

The true secret to success lies in the positive interactions between parent and child. Reinforcement is the key ingredient for working successfully with a child. Once a child's behavior improves, discipline becomes less necessary. Using reinforcing techniques with IA and HM children is critical in helping them overcome their typical low self-esteem. Once youngsters' behavior patterns become positive, they are treated positively, which helps them feel better about themselves.

Reinforcement involves procedures that either maintain or increase behaviors. Conversely, any maintained or increasing behavior is most likely getting reinforced. Often we inadvertently reinforce the bad behaviors we wish to eliminate, which we will later learn to avoid doing. This chapter focuses on how to control reinforcements so that your child will learn new and desired responses.

TYPES OF REINFORCERS

We can divide reinforcers into two broad categories—*social* and *material*. Material reinforcement may be divided into two categories—*activities* and *objects*.

Social reinforcers include personal interactions between you and your child: paying attention, spending time with the child, looking at the child, talking to the child, praising, touching, listening, and just plain showing a response.

Material reinforcers include activities your youngster enjoys: watching television, having free play, going outside, riding a bike, playing games, enjoying special privileges, and attending a ball game. This category also includes prized objects such as toys, favorite foods, money, tokens (check marks, stars, poker chips), and a new bike.

Reasons to Prefer Social Reinforcement

Here is a major difference in the CSP. Unlike most authors who write behavior books on parenting, I strongly endorse the use of social reinforcement over material reinforcement for the following reasons:

1. *Social reinforcement during early childhood is important in developing a close relationship between parent and child.* Positive bonding

cannot occur unless the parent actively reinforces the child for appropriate behaviors. The focus of this book extends beyond controlling behaviors to building strong, loving relationships. I deeply believe that developing this bond lessens the risk of any serious acting out during the teenage years. Some adolescent rebellion will most likely occur, but the severity of it can be curtailed by building a loving relationship.

By building a close relationship, you'll make it easier to teach values to your IA or HM child. Remember, instilling new values is a key element of the CSP. A program based solely on material reinforcement may control behaviors but does little to build relationships.

2. *Material reinforcers generally produce the quickest improvements in behavior, but these improvements often fade rapidly.* We have all observed an improvement in our children's behavior just before the winter holidays, when they hope to earn the toys, dolls, and games advertised on television. By New Year's Eve, the children have tired of the presents and reverted to their preholiday pattern. The incentive is gone.

When the child tires of the reinforcer, it loses its potency for controlling behaviors. This is called the satiation effect. With social reinforcement there is usually no satiation effect to worry about.

3. *Material reinforcers promote a payment expectancy—unless the child earns a material reward, he will not behave.* Several authors dispute this pattern or rationalize that adults are paid for labor and therefore why shouldn't children be paid? I ask: How much are adults paid for work at *home?* We work willingly, lovingly, and voluntarily at home to fulfill our responsibilities to our family. We behave correctly as a sign of courtesy and respect for other family members and not because we get paid. We should expect to develop these same values in our children. They should develop a strong, natural sense of caring and responsibility toward home and family. Teaching these values to our children is more important than simply controlling their behaviors. With social reinforcement, payment expectancy does not become an issue.

4. *Social reinforcement is extremely important for children because it helps them develop a more positive self-image—more self-esteem.* Many parents instinctively, consciously, and consistently praise and socially reinforce their children; unfortunately, many others are unaware of how often they yell at, criticize, punish, or ignore their children.

Youngsters develop their primary attitudes about themselves from how their parents treat them and what their parents say to them. The child who is treated negatively during the early developmental years will not develop a positive self-image. Once early attitudes are locked in—I believe by the age of ten—they are extremely difficult to eradicate.

We should consistently praise our offspring; most of the time they work hard to do the positive things we desire from them.

IA and HM children often have a history of harsh treatment from parents, teachers, and peers. They need social reinforcement more than most children. They need to hear positive things to enhance a more positive self-image. The IA or HM child seems to invite negative reactions. Positive and consistent social reinforcement prevents this kind of problem.

5. *Token economy programs, which are based on material reinforcement, are inappropriate ways to raise children.* Having charts on the wall and giving stars and check marks undermines the normal parent-child social interactions.

If a child is to develop appropriate social skills and a sense of appropriate family interactions, then the family should be a model of normalcy. Lists, charts, and poker chips do not establish a model for normal family behaviors and interactions. Because children are learning patterns of human conduct within the family, it is essential to establish a foundation upon which they can draw as adults when establishing their own families. Adults can be confused about their roles, conduct, and values if their reference point from early life was not normal. Token programs are not normal.

I teach classroom management skills, so I appreciate that token programs can assist in controlling group behaviors in the classroom. But in the home these programs create an inappropriate environment.

PRINCIPLES OF EFFECTIVE REINFORCEMENT

Several basic principles underlie changing our children's behaviors effectively:

1. *Immediate social and material reinforcement is more effective in changing behaviors than delayed reinforcement.* You must reinforce the correct behavior as soon as it occurs if the child is to learn the association between new social skills and behaviors with positive responses from others.

Immediacy is critical during the learning stage of new behaviors. If reinforcement is delayed, children may be confused about what we expect, and the behavior that is occurring at the time of the reinforcement, instead of the behavior we are trying to teach them, will increase. For example, Johnny is told to pick up his toys. He does so quickly, but an hour later, when we praise him for his earlier compliance, he is banging on the table. He will now continue to bang on the table. Reinforcement is incredibly powerful, but if used incorrectly it can work against you.

2. *If reinforcement is to be effective, the parent must reinforce correct responses consistently.* This is extremely important during the learning or acquisition of new appropriate behaviors. In other words, during the learning of new behaviors try to reinforce *each* correct response.

Let me give you a few examples:

You say, "Johnny, please pick up your toys and get ready for dinner." Johnny immediately begins to put his toys away. Reinforce by saying, "Johnny, I'm really proud of you for listening to me and doing as you are told so quickly. I'm very proud of you."

Notice that in our CSP language you are reinforcing compliance to your command.

Or you say, "No Johnny, you may not have candy before we eat." Johnny says "OK" and quietly walks away. If Johnny has a history of temper tantrums, don't let this moment slip by. Say, "Johnny, wait a minute. I want to give you a hug and a kiss. When Dad said no you didn't blow up and you accepted what I said in such a nice way. I love you, son."

Or if you hear Johnny and his sister Mary settle a dispute without fighting, go in the room and say, "Johnny, Mary, I was listening to you two settle your difference in a nice way. Johnny, you asked Mary to play with her keyboard and when she said no you gently told her you'll be careful with it. I'm so proud of you for asking so nicely and without threatening your sister. And Mary, you said no at first, but you listened to what your brother had to say and even changed your mind so he could practice on your keyboard. You didn't whine or cry but instead you handled it like a big girl. I'm so proud of you. I'm so proud of the both of you. I love you."

Training new behavioral patterns requires a lot of work at first, but as these new patterns lock in, our work becomes easier. You will see results much more quickly than you may expect, and the hard-work part does not last very long.

Caregivers must also be consistent in their policies with one another. Both Mom and Dad and every other caregiver must reinforce consistently when an appropriate behavior is being learned. *Whoever is with the child at the moment of a correct response must reinforce that response.*

Several years ago one of my clinic's tutors asked what to do about parents who are so disorganized that they are unable to be consistent. I suggested that the parents consider therapy to learn to be more consistent. Adults who cannot be consistent risk making minimal gains in their work with their children. Sorry folks, but the approach in this book means that you have to work hard to get the desired changes you want in your offspring.

Consistency requires that you reinforce behaviors when the child is in different situations—restaurants, church or synagogue, stores, and so forth. Another good thing about social reinforcement is that you can praise a child anywhere and at any time.

3. *Contingency means that consequences exist for target behaviors.* Reinforcement is given as a consequence of the child's responding correctly; discipline is given as a consequence of the child's not responding correctly. This cause-and-effect formula is the basic foundation for working with IA and HM children. *The more problematic the child, the more strictly we must apply the rules.*

Some authorities (mainly humanistic and Rogerian psychologists) believe that conditional reinforcement is detrimental to a child's psychological development and that children should not have to perform to earn praise. They claim that reinforcement should be unconditional. Embedded in the humanistic writings of Carl Rogers (1951), Thomas Gordon (1970), Eric Fromm (1956), and Abraham Maslow (1962) are concepts and ideas like *conditional reinforcement will hinder the child's natural exploration and learning drive*, and *conditionally reinforced children will grow to be adults who spend their life searching for reinforcement.*

Yes, I believe that children have a natural exploration drive, as these writers proclaim. With conditional reinforcement, however, that drive is more focused and harnessed. Contingent reinforcement is essential for learning new behaviors because it aids and enhances children's natural creative drive rather than blocking it. In other words, it motivates them, which is the key to success with the IA or HM child.

Humanistic psychologists teach that reinforcement should be given no matter what the child's behavior and that we should use unconditional language such as "I love you. You're neat. How wonderful you are."

Many excellent psychological principles and ideas have been developed by humanistic psychologists. But I believe that *both* conditional reinforcement (praise for performance) and unconditional reinforcement (telling the child "I love you") should be practiced abundantly. I am a hugger and a kisser with my children. I reinforce them unconditionally—a lot—for just being my children. Children who are abundantly reinforced will be more comfortable and secure about themselves and thus will be *less* likely to spend their lives searching for approval.

CONDITIONALITY OF REINFORCEMENT

Here is a little secret: *all* reinforcement is conditional and contingent. Whether reinforcement is intended to be conditional or unconditional, *any* interaction with a child reinforces whatever behavior is going on at that time. It is not a matter of what is said; it is a matter of timing. If you make contact with the child, you are reinforcing that child at that moment. Here's an example:

MOM: Johnny, please pick up your toys.
JOHNNY: You don't love me!
MOM: I love you. It's your behavior I don't like.

On the surface this seems to be a healthy interaction with a child. The reality is this: Mother is inadvertently reinforcing the poor-me statement (You don't love me). By interacting with her child, she is reinforcing the behavior that precedes the interaction. The child makes an association between the verbalization and her attention. If this continues, the parent is likely to see an increase in poor-me verbalizations, while noncompliance remains at the same level. *Timing is the key.*

In our approach, as you'll learn in the chapter on discipline, if Johnny frequently uses poor-me statements to manipulate, then consequences should be firmly and immediately implemented. I'm reluctant to introduce the idea of time out here, because in the CSP it has been redesigned to deal with the IA or HM child, and it is best to carefully read the chapter. However, I'll digress in this instance for teaching purposes. Johnny engaged in two target behaviors in rapid succession: he was noncompliant and made a poor-me statement. Therefore, the sequence of rigorous parent-child interaction necessitates not reinforcing these behaviors and instead disciplining them immediately as follows:

MOM: Johnny, please pick up your toys.
JOHNNY: You don't love me!
MOM: (in a firm voice) Go to time out!

After time out, this is what should happen:

MOM: Johnny, you may come out of time out. (Johnny walks up to her.) Why did you go to time out?
JOHNNY: Because I didn't pick up my toys.
MOM: And what else?
JOHNNY: Because I said you don't love me.
MOM: What are you supposed to do?
JOHNNY: Pick up my toys.
MOM: Good. Now go do it. (Johnny turns toward the room his toys are in.) Thank you for listening, Johnny. (Her statement immediately reinforces correct compliance.)

We are interacting contingently with our children all the time. Unfortunately, much of this interaction is negative. At home and at school, when children are quiet and being well behaved, we ignore them. When they do or say something inappropriate, we give them our attention—the negative kind.

If you wish to make unconditional reinforcing statements to your child, make them while your child is behaving well. When my children are sitting quietly playing, reading, or watching TV, I often hug them and say, "I love you." By not giving them attention when they misbehave, I deliberately avoid inadvertently reinforcing unwanted or undesired behavior.

Caregivers—mainly parents and teachers—are judicious about contingent punishment but are lacking in contingent reinforcement. Again, the secret of success is not the punishment; it is the reinforcement.

USE OF SOCIAL REINFORCEMENT

When socially reinforcing a behavior, use descriptive statements such as these:

"I like the way you're sitting at the dinner table. You're being quiet and asking for things in a nice way."

When Johnny brings you his homework after completion say, "You did a beautiful job on your homework. Your writing is nice and neat, just the way Mommy showed you."

"Johnny, I'm glad that you picked up your toys when Mommy asked you, without making a fuss. I'm very proud of you."

These statements should serve as positive reminders of what the child is doing correctly and exactly what behavior is needed to earn the caregiver's approval. Positive descriptive statements should be used by all caregivers, including parents, teachers, and grandparents.

Parents use descriptive statements all the time, but usually in a negative way, such as:

"Why didn't you pick up your toys like I asked you?"

"Why don't you ever listen to Mommy?"

"Stop making those sounds at the dinner table. I want you to sit quietly and keep your mouth shut."

"Your paper is sloppy. Look at that letter L. How many times do I have to show you how to do it right?"

In other words we wait for children to misbehave and then we interact with them negatively by yelling and describing what they did wrong. Negative statements are the predominant way parents and teachers treat children, and sadly it is the predominant way we treat IA and HM children. This pattern proves counterproductive for children who should be developing a positive self-image.

Have you noticed that misbehavior often gets gradually worse until we explode? For example, Johnny may kick the table leg and we try to ignore him. Then he hits his sister—*then* we explode. To prevent escalation of misbehaviors, learn vigilance. Use positive description statements before the child does anything wrong. An example is, "Johnny, you're sitting so quietly tonight at the table. I'm proud of you." Do this before he starts banging on the table. Reinforce the child as early in the sequence as possible.

One thing to avoid when reinforcing socially is *talking to your children in an exaggerated, childish manner.* While saccharine or falsely sweet statements do get the attention of the very young child, they also model inappropriate social behavior. The child will probably imitate this verbal pattern, and then other children may respond with ridicule and ostracism, which, in turn, can be very painful and scarring. Speak to young children in a clear, warm, and caring way. Be natural.

Use of Social Reinforcement to Shape Complex Skills

Shaping is a reinforcing technique that helps motivate children to learn new skills, and motivation is the key to success with the IA or HM child. Shaping breaks a complex behavior or skill down into a number of small steps, making learning easier. Gains in each of the steps earn a descriptive praise. Figure 5.1 illustrates how a behavior is shaped by reinforcement.

Here's an example of shaping:

We want five-year-old Danny to make his bed each morning. First, we observe what he can do without help (this is base level), then we praise (reinforce) him for his effort, no matter how far from perfect his initial attempt may be. Second, we show Danny how to do the next step, such as pulling the cover evenly over the bed. The

Figure 5.1. Shaping a Behavior.

child then practices this until he gets it right. When Danny has mastered steps 1 and 2, we praise him.

We reserve reinforcement until Danny masters the most recent step. Step 3 may be tucking the bedspread under the pillow. Step 4 may be smoothing the bedspread over the pillows.

We do not have to teach the child all the steps in one day. Yes, shaping does require effort on your part, but once your child learns how to make the bed, you'll never have to do it for him again. Isn't that wonderful?

Shaping complex behavior and self-help skills holds several important benefits: Children learn to share the family responsibilities, which helps them feel important. They learn to do tasks independently, without prompting, coaxing, and relying on you for help almost all of the time. These are crucial elements of the CSP.

Use of Shaping to Combat Dependency

Remember the target behavior of dependency? Well, skill building reduces task, cognitive, and emotional dependency. Furthermore, youngsters learn to take pride in themselves for successfully accomplishing increasingly complex skills, and this fosters a positive self-image. Start this process when your child is young, and I doubt he will ever be diagnosed as IA or HM.

The use of shaping may hold important implications for adult life. Many skills are never taught by parents or teachers because of the time and trouble it would take to do so. I urge you to teach your children as many skills as possible so they can develop self-confidence and independence. Add increasingly complex skills as they get older: how to cook, how to wash clothes, how to fix a light switch, how to repair a car, and so on.

Yes, being patient is sometimes difficult when children make mistakes. Yes, often doing the task ourselves is faster and easier than preparing our youngsters to assume the responsibility. Building skills and self-confidence and improving independent functioning are far more important goals than efficiency.

Use of Shaping in the Classroom

If you are a teacher, are you using shaping as a classroom technique for learning new skills? Are you using shaping with your own children as well as with your students? Do you as a teacher judiciously and consistently use social reinforcement in shaping complex concepts? Do you praise students for what they do correctly and well? Do you reinforce each student equally throughout the academic day? In other words, is shaping skills an everyday event for you?

If so, you are most likely an excellent teacher. Some teachers may complain that actively reinforcing all children each day is too much to ask for. I don't think so. All teachers need to do is walk around the classroom while the children are on task and touch their shoulder, praise them, and smile at them for their efforts and for their skill improvements. Doesn't this create a more positive environment for all children?

Praising the IA or HM child for effort is an important motivating tool. When stopping to help students, the teacher can also prompt them on the next step while praising them for having improved a skill by one or more steps. This requires only a few seconds with each child.

Remember that trouble in school is the main reason IA and HM children are referred for therapy. Also recall that these children are not motivated to perform well in school. Bluntly stated, they hate school. A positive teacher using shaping techniques is crucial in getting these children to like school, that is, to motivate them to want to do well. If a child becomes positively motivated to perform well in school, the IA or HM patterns will disappear.

USE OF MATERIAL REINFORCEMENT

I have rarely had to use material programs with children below the age of twelve because correctly applying social reinforcement produces such excellent results. Sometimes, however, material reinforcers are useful for controlling behaviors that do not occur in the parent's presence. Most frequently this means school performance—one of the most important concerns of parents with an IA or HM child.

Because 20 percent of IA and HM cases may require additional intervention because of no improvement in school, material reinforcers become useful. Later in the book (see Chapter Ten) you'll be learning how to help this 20 percent with a school program. Therefore, this is a good point at which to outline some easy-to-understand guidelines for a material program that we'll use in that chapter.

The principles of immediacy, consistency, and contingency that apply to social reinforcement apply to material programs as well. Here are additional principles reserved specifically for objects and activities:

1. *Identify what your child finds reinforcing.* Do not assume that you know what is reinforcing to a child. Just because you like ice

cream doesn't mean your child does. Through observation, determine what objects and activities your youngster prefers.

I recall one couple whose little girl was a terror. A head trauma at birth had left her brain-damaged and retarded. They had looked for help for years but in vain. They said, "Nothing is reinforcing to our child."

I disagreed. All children—even the seriously disturbed—have a wide variety of reinforcing objects and activities. I asked the parents to observe their child carefully for clues, and a week later they returned with a short but sufficient list of reinforcers—chewing gum, wearing a favorite old T-shirt, and listening to the radio at bedtime. You see? There is always something. With this list we began the program, and sure enough it was successful.

2. *To avoid lapses due to satiation, update and monitor on a continuous and ongoing basis.* Material reinforcers eventually lose effectiveness because of overuse or overexposure (the satiation mentioned earlier). What may be reinforcing early in the program may later no longer attract the child and should be replaced with something more effective.

Some parents combat satiation by removing a particular reinforcer for a while in the hope of maintaining its effectiveness. As you probably already know, when you deprive a child of an object or activity, the youngster finds it desirable. For example, if you do not allow your child to use her bicycle, it probably won't bother her for a few days. Eventually she will most likely begin requesting it more and more. At that point, having use of her bicycle will be useful for controlling a behavior because it will have regained importance to your child.

The laws in many states require that some reinforcers may not be withheld. Food is an example. As a guideline, never remove or deprive children of a reinforcer that is life-sustaining, such as food, water, shelter, or clothing. These are called primary reinforcers. All other reinforcers—a bicycle, a football, a favorite doll—are called secondary reinforcers and can be useful in controlling undesirable behaviors.

3. *If a child fails to get one reinforcer, he is not allowed to substitute something else in its place.* I have found that a program works better and faster when this principle is in effect.

This case will clarify the principle. Because seven-year-old Michael dawdled every morning, he missed the bus and his mother had to drive him to school. In IA and HM children dawdling is very common. This made his mother late for work. Waking him up earlier did not remedy the situation. Yelling, pleading, and threatening did not help either. IA or HM children are excellent at getting your dander up

Michael loved to ride his bicycle, so we gave him the contingency that if he was ready for school on time, exactly at 7:45 A.M., he could ride his bike after school from 3:30 to 5:00. If he failed to be on time in the morning, he would not be allowed to ride his bike or do anything else—no substitutions—on that day during those ninety minutes. This meant that from 3:30 to 5:00 Michael was deprived of contact with friends, phone calls, and most especially, homework, which meant he had to do it all later in the evening and miss his favorite TV show. Some readers may think this is a bit harsh or strict. But remember, the techniques in the CSP are designed for the IA or HM child. This means that we want to change inappropriate behaviors to appropriate behaviors in the briefest possible time.

If we want Michael to change fast and avoid any pressure to put him on Ritalin, these rigorous techniques are sometimes called for. However, in this program each day is a fresh start. This means that Michael can make choices: be ready and on time the next day and be allowed to ride his bike, be late again and not ride his bike, or get his homework done early.

If Michael can substitute other reinforcers during this time period, we neutralize the stringency or rigor of the CSP. If Michael can't ride his bike but can play with his video games, the consequences to him are meaningless.

The removal of homework is also important because if he completes his homework in this time period, he's free later to pursue fun activities. In my work with IA and HM children I have found that allowing them to do their homework when an activity has been lost indeed neutralizes the effectiveness of the CSP.

The IA or HM child is out of control; strong, firm intervention is called for. Stringency is what makes the CSP work. The faster a child changes, the faster he receives an abundance of positive material and social reinforcements. The faster he improves, the sooner peers and adults like him, which means the faster his world becomes more positive. I prefer this stringency to the use of drugs or corporal punishment, or to allowing these children to continue suffering the pain of ostracism and repeated failures.

Michael's mother did not permit him to swap activities, which would have neutralized the program's effectiveness. The first week this was put into effect, Michael was on time each day and he has been ever since. This was accomplished without resorting to Ritalin.

4. *Do not offer to buy the child something special if he improves a behavior.* Getting a new bicycle for good grades teaches youngsters about bribery and extortion. Instead, *we require them to earn the reinforcers that are already part of their environment or part of their daily routine.*

Examples of natural reinforcers are watching one hour of television at night, talking to friends on the telephone, playing touch football with friends, going outside for free play after school for an hour and a half, and eating a favorite dessert after dinner.

Each of these can be useful when we have to deal with some very important behaviors. In fact, these reinforcers should be used if a school program becomes necessary. In that program we use a daily report card; the day's grades determine the use of these reinforcers, with no substitutions. Each day is a new day with a new report card. Therefore, the IA or HM child can make a decision to perform well and behave correctly that day or lose the reinforcers.

5. *Social reinforcement must also be given abundantly whenever the child's performance is correct.* Even when using material reinforcers, we must still reinforce socially. Material programs will fail quickly unless correct behavior is also rewarded with a praise, a hug, a kiss, and so on. Remember this as a cardinal rule for all behavioral methods: The real success is in the social reinforcement.

IMPORTANCE OF CONSISTENT AND CONTINGENT REINFORCEMENT

I know you're eager to learn about discipline, and I promise we'll get there. Consistent social reinforcement, however, is the key to success. Without it, no form of discipline will work. In fact, nothing will work.

When actively reinforcing behaviors you'll begin to see incorrect target behaviors subside and new appropriate behaviors begin to emerge. Without knowing how to correctly discipline, the changes won't be substantial, because it is the combination of reinforcement with appropriate discipline that is essential to getting the complete change we're striving for. However, most of the families I've worked with begin socially reinforcing right after this lesson and then appear for the next session smiling. They begin to see changes right away, which means *no Ritalin for their child* is becoming a reality.

6

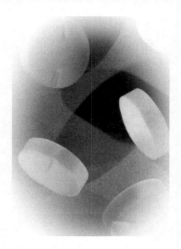

PUNISHMENT

In parenting our children many of us rely more on punishment than reinforcement. Often we are not aware that we do this. In this chapter we will review why the reliance on punishment with children can have negative and defeating effects. Punishing IA or HM (ADD or ADHD) children can actually contribute to their behavioral and cognitive patterns. We will explore the reasons we must no longer rely on punishment if we are to get IA and HM children off Ritalin and why the development of alternate methods of discipline in the CSP has been so essential.

PUNISHMENT CAN MAKE MATTERS WORSE

Because parents are often so eager to learn punishment techniques, I must remind them that the key for changing children's behavior successfully is reinforcement. Positive social reinforcement in the form of praise and hugs is far more powerful than punishment for the child's mental, emotional, and behavioral development.

Unfortunately, many of us rely almost exclusively on punishment when dealing with our children.

Ask yourself if you are a consistent reinforcer with your child. Or do you rely on screaming, yelling, and hitting to control your child's behavior? If yours is an IA or HM child, the invitation to frequently punish can be considerable. I know this is hard to face, but try to be objective. Punishing is such an easy trap to fall into.

Consider the question, Has it worked? Over time, has your IA or HM child improved or has her behavior either stayed the same or perhaps even gotten worse? Have you noticed that you've been punishing more frequently and more intensely?

Not only does punishment not work very well but if the primary method of dealing with children is negative, don't be surprised when, as adolescents, they discover their power, rebel, and want to stay away from you. Punishment damages relationships and does little to make your child warm and loving. In fact, frequent punishment is instrumental in developing severe alienation between parent and child.

PUNISHMENT AND ITS EFFECTS ON CHILDREN

Before we look at the effects and characteristics of punishment, let's define the term more precisely. *Punishment* is the application of an aversive (painful) stimulus, such as yelling and hitting, to decrease a behavior. Now let's see how punishment affects children.

Brief, Temporary Results

Mild-to-moderate punishment suppresses behavior only temporarily. When the punishment stops, the behavior returns—perhaps not immediately but it returns. Parents often say to me, "I yell at him. I scream at him. I hit him. I turn around, and he's doing it again. What is wrong with him?"

Punishment is a suppressing tool. It does not teach new behaviors. Remove it and up pops the old behavior day after day. Reinforcement does teach new behaviors. It is the key for motivating and shaping improved behaviors.

Habitual Use by the Punisher

Punishment suppresses a misbehavior quickly. These instantaneous results are reinforcing to adults. When we yell, "Keep quiet!" and our child instantly obeys, we are training ourselves to rely on yelling. Why? Because it is immediately reinforcing to us. The child's being temporarily quiet is more powerful for us than delayed but more lasting results. Recall that we discussed this principle of immediacy in the last chapter. We are not discouraged by the fact that the misbehaviors we punish keep coming back; the instantaneous results cause us to develop the habit of punishing. Over time, punishing our child begins to feel comfortable and natural.

Reinforcing our child's good behavior works more slowly but the change is permanent. Offering reinforcement can feel abnormal, unnatural, and uncomfortable to us simply because we are not used to doing it.

Bad Side Effects

Severe punishment, consistently applied, may permanently suppress some target behaviors. The major side effects of severe punishment, however, actually make matters worse.

One of the side effects of severe and consistent punishment is anxiety. A child's feeling nervous and tense counteracts our goals. We want our children to learn new and appropriate behaviors. The nervous child does not learn well; tension interferes with new learning, which means it becomes increasingly difficult to teach the IA or HM child new behaviors. Then, in turn, parents become even more upset with their child because he is not learning well, which means they punish even more. Not a very good cycle to get into, is it?

The nervous child also makes more mistakes than a calm one, which in time leads to more parental frustration and often to still more punishment. Furthermore, the nervous child tends to be agitated and hyper—the very pattern we're trying to eliminate.

One of the key features of children who don't pay attention is that they are nervous; they have trouble sitting still and paying attention. So we call them hyperactive or highly misbehaving. Parents who punish help cause this pattern in the first place. This is a terribly negative cycle that must be stopped. If you yell at and hit your child, stop it right now. Otherwise, nothing in this book will work for you. And learn to talk without yelling. Talk in a natural tone.

Emotional Problems

Severely punished children can become emotionally and socially withdrawn because they believe that interacting with people is a painful experience. Seeking to escape and avoid their cruel environment, they may hide in their room or roam the streets. In my experience, such an isolated, withdrawn child can get into serious trouble, commit serious misdeeds such as vandalism, and become prone to suicide attempts. He is also vulnerable to involvement with drugs or alcohol, which deadens the pain deep inside.

I recall one child, Joseph, whose parents believed that punishing was *the* way to raise a child. They confused punishment with being strict, which is to set firm limits on behavior. Yelling and spanking were a daily occurrence. The punishment continued through Joseph's teen years. He developed a stutter. He became a very anxious young man. In conversation he kept his head down, not looking the other person in the eye.

When Joseph went to college he found a way to ease some of his nervousness—alcohol. He quickly became an excessive drinker, in fact an alcoholic. Joseph's parents realized too late that their punitive philosophy was completely wrong.

If severe and consistent punishment is coupled with neglect, the odds are slim that an emotionally healthy child will emerge from the household. A child from this environment will most likely be highly anxious and very lonely—in other words, an emotional wreck.

Aggression

What we model is what our children learn. Parents who hit, yell, or shake their child are modeling aggression. The child learns to use aggressive responses to handle his frustrations.

In addition, severely punished children are likely to become aggressive because they are filled with anger and hostility. The likelihood exists that they will lash out at anyone in their way. If they try to suppress their deep anger, they may someday explode inside, lose control, and hurt someone.

Recently I have been working with the case of William, whose father is physically and mentally abusive. In dealing with this father I warned him that his thirteen-year-old son was so filled with rage that he could very well strike back. In other words I told the father that he was in danger. I asked the father to enter into therapy to deal with his own rage. He told me that he didn't come to see me for himself and that all he wanted from me was to fix his child. I diplomatically tried to tell him how his behavior was affecting his child, but I guess I didn't do a very good job; he never returned. I pray that what I predicted will never become true.

On many occasions I have witnessed parents either spanking children or hitting them across the face while saying, "Where have you learned such behavior? We don't teach you to hit someone!"

The modeling of aggression does not have to be directed toward the child in order for it to be learned. It can be directed to other family members or even to inanimate objects. One father I worked with lost his temper frequently in the car in the presence of his children; he pounded on the dashboard, screamed, and cursed. What do you think he was teaching his children?

An occasional flare-up is normal, and parents need not feel guilty for occasionally overreacting to stress. Frequent flare-ups, however, are inappropriate modeling. Simply stated, aggressive children come from aggressive families.

Adaptation to Pain

Over time, children can adapt to intense levels of pain. In order to control a child over the years, parents are forced to yell ever louder and hit harder. Eventually the child no longer responds to the pain, as tolerance levels escalate.

Even though the youngster is adapting to pain, all the previously mentioned side effects will still occur, and feelings will be locked inside. Youngsters will not communicate with highly punitive parents.

When a child has learned to tune out, as the highly punished child has, he may appear empty-headed, obtuse, oblivious, and non-responsive. He may miss environmental cues, hide in a fantasy world, or shut off his brain and hardly think at all. *This is another important way to contribute to the development and evolution of an IA or HM child.* In other words, this adds up to children who don't pay attention or think.

If withdrawal is due to a punitive home environment, a psychotherapist will have to work with the parents to help them understand how detrimental their frequent tirades are to their child.

Bad Effects on Punisher

Yelling and hitting are inappropriate ways to express angry feelings. Some authors advocate *catharsis*—acting out one's feelings as a means of expressing and venting pent-up emotions. But research has repeatedly shown that expressions of anger and aggression lead to more expressions of anger and aggression and, if continued over a long period of time, angry expression becomes a habit.

A parent may experience a temporary release of emotional pressure, but in the long run it is not emotionally healthy and can ruin relationships. Did you know that people prone to anger are also prone to heart attacks? Your anger is hurting you. One of the most frequent problems that leads to broken marriages is when one partner has frequent outbursts of anger.

Try having a tirade in front of your boss. You won't do it, will you? Most of the time we express our anger in a setting we perceive as safe—usually at home. We do this, falsely believing we can get away with it when targeting our children or our spouse. But you may be surprised when they turn on you.

A healthier alternative is to express feelings assertively. Teach your child to say, "Mommy (Daddy), I'm mad at you because you're not listening to me!" instead of having temper tantrums. Assertiveness vents the child's feelings constructively. You can find numerous books on assertiveness. I recommend that if you, as a parent, become angry often, then you need to read several of these books.

Reinforcement of Undesired Behaviors

Punishment may have the effect of maintaining or increasing undesirable behaviors. When parents yell at or hit their child, remember the list on social reinforcement I told you to mark, and note the following:

Social Element	*Reinforcement*	
	Yes	No
Are the parents paying attention?	✔	
Are they spending time with the child?	✔	
Are they talking to the child?	✔	
Are they looking at the child?	✔	
Are they listening to the child?		✔
Are they touching the child?	✔	
Are they praising the child?		✔
Are they showing a response?	✔	

Note that for yelling and hitting, six out of eight elements provide social reinforcement. When we examine this list, we realize
that what seems like punishment to us may actually be reinforcing
to the child!

Recall parents who say, "I yell at him, I hit him, and he does it
again! What's wrong with that kid?" What's wrong is that the parents are reinforcing the very behaviors they don't want. Many IA
and HM behaviors are inadvertently reinforced in this way.

Remember that any behavior being maintained or increased is
being reinforced. In other words, we are reinforcing the very behaviors we are trying to get rid of. As a matter of fact, children learn to
misbehave just to get attention, even if it is negative and punitive
attention. Children are not aware of doing this. Now do you see
why target behaviors keep coming back?

Punishment Becomes Reinforcing

We can look at social stimulation three ways: (1) as positive stimulation (+), (2) as no stimulation (0 or zero), or (3) as negative
stimulation (−).

Research shows that children (and adults) hate zero stimulation.
Zero stimulation means conditions in which the child receives neither positive stimulation (reinforcement), that is, no hugs, kisses,
or praises, nor negative stimulation (punishment) such as yelling or
hitting. Oddly, if positive stimulation (reinforcement) is absent,
children will seek unpleasant stimulation (punishment) rather than
no stimulation. *Zero stimulation is a condition that children seek to avoid
the most.* If the parent is not positively reinforcing the child, then
where does she turn for stimulation? Right! To the negative forms
of attention, that is, punishment. Much of the IA or HM child's
behavior is to seek some form of attention. If reinforcement is lacking, she'll actually seek punishment to get attention.

In the next chapters you will learn effective methods of discipline—methods that really work. Notice the last item, that children
mostly dislike an absence of stimulation. Therefore, psychologists

have developed discipline methods based on zero stimulation: ignoring, sending to time out, and removing reinforcement. These methods not only work extremely well but they have none of the drawbacks we just reviewed.

Now let's go to the following chapters to learn exactly what these methods of discipline are.

7

BEGINNING TO LEARN DISCIPLINE

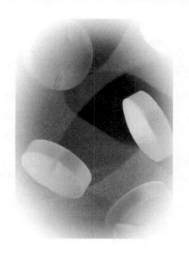

In the last chapter we learned that punishment is not only detrimental to the IA or HM child but may actually contribute to the development of IA or HM behaviors. Therefore, more effective forms of discipline that quickly produce permanent changes are needed if we're going to keep the IA or HM child off Ritalin. In the preceding chapter I discussed how children dislike and avoid zero stimulation—the absence of reinforcement or punishment. This information helped psychologists develop discipline techniques based on zero stimulation that are not only highly effective but lack the detrimental effects of traditional forms of punishment.

The three methods we will be discussing are *ignoring, time out,* and *reinforcement removal (RR)*. Ignoring will be discussed in this chapter. Time out, which has been specifically redesigned for the IA or HM child, will be discussed in Chapter Eight. Reinforcement removal will be discussed in Chapter Nine; it is a stronger discipline technique.

We'll begin this chapter by defining what *discipline* means and what criteria are necessary for it to be effective. Some forms of discipline can be unintended traps that can work against our goals of helping the IA or HM child and ultimately keeping him off Ritalin. Therefore, you'll learn what these traps are and how to avoid them.

THE TREATMENT SEQUENCE

Before beginning the discussion of discipline, I want to emphasize the sequence to use in dealing with IA or HM children.

First, actively reinforce all forms of positive behavior. If IA or HM patterns continue, try reasoning with your child. At a quiet time discuss your concerns about specific target behaviors. For example, you could say, "Tommy, whenever I tell you to do something are you aware that you ignore me, or you get mad and talk back to me? Sometimes you even lose your temper. Honey, I'd like you to learn to talk to me in a nice way. I promise I'll try to carefully listen to what you have to say but I can't promise I'll always agree with you."

When reason fails we begin activating the discipline techniques.

Ignoring—the mildest form of discipline—is only useful for the mildest forms of misbehaviors and is covered in this chapter.

Time out is the most frequently used and successful method and is used if reasoning fails or if the behaviors are too strong for ignoring. Time out in the Caregivers' Skills Program has been specifically designed for IA and HM children, so read the chapter with considerable care.

Finally, reinforcement removal (in psychology this is formally called response cost) is used for behaviors that are highly resistant to treatment, for example, lying and more severe misbehaviors such as aggression.

THE CRITERIA OF EFFECTIVE DISCIPLINE

Before discussing specific methods of discipline it is important to review, in the sections that follow, the ingredients of the criteria that are necessary if discipline is really going to work.

Immediacy

Discipline should be applied *immediately* following a misbehavior. Recall that this rule also applies to reinforcement. Ideally, the child should be disciplined while the misbehavior is occurring, so an association is made between misbehavior and consequences. If discipline is delayed, its administration may occur when the child is behaving acceptably. Consequently, the child may learn to associate discipline with proper behavior, which can be very confusing.

We must be able to correct misbehavior that occurs outside the home, so I will teach you how to discipline at Grandma's house or at the supermarket without embarrassing your child. Let's look at an example.

My children and I were visiting their grandmother. Their aunt was also present with her four children. My son Kevin got a bit rough with one of his younger cousins. Not wishing to embarrass him but also wanting to deal with his misconduct I quietly told him to come over to me. I whispered in his ear, "I want you to go sit on Grandma's bed for time out." He did so for ten minutes and when he came out he whispered to me what he had done wrong. I asked him how he should be playing, which he correctly answered, and then I let him resume his play. He learned that even at Grandma's he must remember how to behave.

The rule is to meet the requirement for immediacy as best we can.

Consistency

Discipline cannot be sporadic or haphazard if parents hope to see improvement in their children's behaviors and attitudes. It must be consistent. This rule also applied to reinforcement. Parental inconsistency is one of the most frequent problems in dealing with children. In addition, be aware that IA and HM children require even more consistency than most children. Being inconsistent confuses them, so they have trouble knowing what is right or wrong. This means they can't think correctly—the trademark of IA and HM children. Let's look at another example.

Mark was an extreme IA-HM child. His mother had a history of being very inconsistent with him. She let numerous behaviors slip past her and then would scream at him for something minor, like giggling at the dinner table. She and her husband went through training, but Mark's mother continued to be inconsistent, resulting in minimal improvements. I suggested therapy for her. Once she completed therapy she was able to be very consistent, which finally resulted in remarkable changes in Mark.

To get results with the IA or HM child, you will have to work hard if you wish to be consistent. Of course you'd prefer to drop your child at the therapist's office for an hour each week and enjoy wonderful results. Sorry. It just doesn't work that way.

No Nervousness, No Humiliation

Discipline should not produce tension or anxiety within the child. Physical punishment, which does that, is ruled out.

A spanking, a paddling, or a smack across the face can be degrading and humiliating. To this day I feel the humiliation of those occasions as a child. This is exactly what an IA or HM child who already has low self-esteem does not need.

Similarly, yelling can be detrimental. Frequent yelling can impair the parent-child relationship. It can also make your child very nervous. If you yell often, watch out when your child becomes an adolescent. He has learned from you how to yell, and your teenager will yell back. Also, please remember that frequent yelling teaches a child to tune out, which is exactly what we don't want the IA or HM child to learn.

No Unintended Reinforcement

The best methods of discipline require as little person-to-person interaction as possible. As we review discipline techniques you'll learn that only one sentence is permitted to initiate the discipline, which is usually "Go to time out!" Any additional interaction inadvertently reinforces the behavior you're working on. You must minimize the risk of socially reinforcing the very behavior you're trying to eliminate.

ACTIVELY REINFORCE
THE GOOD BEHAVIORS

No matter what method of discipline is employed and no matter how effective the research says it is, no long-lasting gains will occur unless parents reinforce the child for good behaviors. This includes deliberate praise for specific improvement and unconditional expressions of love and caring when the child is behaving well.

Even though many parents work full-time, they must make the time for talking to and for having fun with their children. All children must have individual attention; otherwise, any program is doomed to failure. Without abundant reinforcement we will not achieve the end result we hope for: a well-behaved and well-motivated child. Such a youngster comes only from a loving home.

ZERO STIMULATION:
THE MOST EFFECTIVE DISCIPLINE

I have stated that the most aversive environment for children is one in which there is no stimulation. Zero stimulation means that contact with material or social reinforcers is almost completely eliminated and all aversive and punishing contact is removed. Zero stimulation means that the environment around the child is as boring as possible. Because punishment does not work, psychologists have developed three effective methods of discipline that employ zero stimulation (boredom). These methods get the best results without the drawbacks or side effects we just discussed. (Isn't it interesting that boredom can get better results than punishment?)

The three methods we will look at that approximate zero stimulation are ignoring, time out, and reinforcement removal (RR).

Ignoring

Ignoring, which means removing social reinforcement, is useful only
for very mild target behaviors—those you can tolerate without losing control. If you lose control you will run into several traps that
can make matters worse, so keep in mind that ignoring is only useful for extremely mild misbehaviors. *Mild* is a very subjective term
and means behavior you can usually ignore. If you can't ignore it or
if it annoys you, it isn't mild.

The Traps in Ignoring

Figure 7.1 shows the pattern that can unfold in the level of behaviors before and after ignoring begins. These traps also apply whenever social or material reinforcement is removed, either in time out
or RR. If you follow me step by step, the graph's meaning becomes
clearer. At each step, if you do the wrong thing, there are traps that
can actually worsen behavior.

Begin at point 1, greatly condensed, which indicates the learning of behaviors and misbehaviors over many years. Many target
behaviors are learned slowly in the beginning, followed by an accel-
eration of learning, and finally a tapering off of the learning process.
This is called the learning curve.

The Worsening of Behavior

The dashed line at point 2 shows where the ignoring begins.
Can you see that the target behavior worsens (point 3) immediately following the beginning of ignoring? For example, if Mary
uses crying in a manipulative way when you try to ignore her, she'll
start crying louder. Let's say she demands a piece of candy while
you are shopping in the grocery store. You answer, "No, sweetheart.
No candy before dinner." Mary then begins to cry. You turn away
from her to ignore her crying. You know what comes next: she

Figure 7.1. What Happens When a Target Behavior Is Ignored

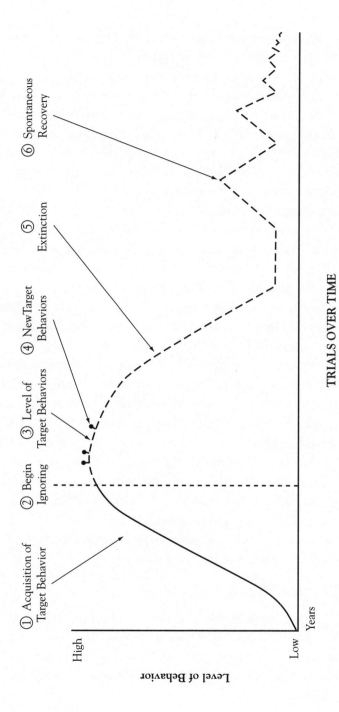

starts crying loud enough for the whole store full of people to hear her. Is it tempting to give in just to avoid the embarrassment? If you do, Mary may stop crying at that point but guess what she'll learn to do the next time she goes shopping with Mother: cry louder.

Two other examples of target behaviors include banging on the dining-room table and nagging. When any of these behaviors become intense, most parents lose patience and yell at, or perhaps spank, the child. Then, as you now know, the parent is inadvertently reinforcing the undesired behavior. The child learns that by behaving more intensely, she wins attention. What did Mary learn?

To avoid this trap, the parent must use the *100 percent rule*, which means that once ignoring is begun, it must be implemented 100 percent of the time or matters will be made worse. Mary's mother should not give in. She should let Mary cry, even though it's embarrassing, until Mary gets tired and eventually stops. Otherwise, Mary will learn to cry louder and louder during every shopping trip in order to get candy.

If Johnny nags you to buy a small toy from the toy machine, which is always placed at the entrance of grocery stores, and you try to ignore him, he'll nag more incessantly. Give in and you've taught him to nag more relentlessly to get his way. If Billy bangs on the dinner table and you ignore it for a while, resulting in his banging harder, the odds are that eventually you'll resort to yelling at him to stop. You have then taught him how to win at getting attention at the dinner table: bang louder. Understanding this may help you see that ignoring can only be used for much milder forms of behavior. Can you completely ignore any of these three behaviors? If you can't, there are stronger ways to discipline.

Emerging of New Behaviors

If the parent is able to ignore the target behavior 100 percent of the time, the child will then try several *new* target behaviors that may not have been in the child's initial repertoire of misbehaviors (point 4). For example, Billy may deliberately knock over a glass of water or hit his brother, or claim to be sick. Mary may have a temper tantrum. Johnny may kick you. Thus, a second trap can now occur. The parent, again losing patience, may yell or spank. The result will be to reinforce new problem behaviors. This will only wind up increasing the total number of target behaviors.

The solution to this dilemma is to adhere to the 100 percent rule of ignoring for the milder misbehaviors or to use stronger discipline techniques for the more severe behaviors, which you will shortly learn how to do.

The Return of Behavior

If the parent is able to control his frustration, the initial target behavior will finally begin to *extinguish* (point 5), that is, it will go away.

Don't sigh with relief yet! The problem is not quite solved. The behavior may remain extinguished for a few days or even a few weeks. However, it can suddenly reemerge, probably less intensely, as shown at point 6 on the graph. If the parent believes the problem has been solved, he'll probably get angry, scream, and spank— once again inadvertently reinforcing the target behavior, which will return to its original level. To make matters worse, now the behavior will be resistant to *extinction,* meaning that you have taught the child to wait in order to get her way. Eventually the day will come when Mary once again cries in the store, Johnny will try nagging again, and Billy will try banging on the dinner table. If their parents give in, each child will have learned that, with persistence, their parent will break down. A good lesson from this last trap is that "inconsistency breeds persistency."

This process will most likely occur several times. To avoid the reinforcement trap, you must follow the 100 percent rule. Ignore completely, and the behavior will finally extinguish completely, as shown at point 6.

As you can see, ignoring is very inefficient and slow. It requires infinite patience and works only against attention-seeking misbehavior.

If a behavior is not attention seeking, such as playing a video game, which is a self-stimulating game and not conducted to get attention, then ignoring is useless. If you cannot be patient when dealing with a particular target behavior, then do not use ignoring.

Avoid Competing Reinforcement

For ignoring to work, reinforcement from other sources must be removed. For example, if you are ignoring Erica's behavior while her brother and sister are laughing uncontrollably at her or while your spouse is trying to talk sense into Erica, ignoring will not work.

Reinforce Correct Behavior

In order for ignoring to work, it is essential that you actively and deliberately reinforce the child's correct responses. The combination of ignoring the incorrect target behavior while reinforcing the correct behavior is called *differential reinforcement*. Give your children the attention they need in a positive way when they are behaving well and ignore them when they misbehave.

Mary's mother, when beginning shopping, should lean over, hug and kiss Mary and say, "You're being such a good girl. You didn't ask for candy and you're not crying. After dinner tonight you can have an extra piece of cake." When passing the toy machine Johnny's dad should say, "Son, you didn't nag for a toy. You remembered our talk about how expensive those toys can be. I'm proud of you." "Billy, you are sitting so quietly tonight at the dinner table. You are so considerate. That makes me feel so good."

TRAPS IN ALL FORMS OF DISCIPLINE

Each of these traps can occur with all forms of discipline. Therefore, you'll be learning much more powerful methods that, when applied correctly, can avoid each trap. Even though ignoring is only useful for the mildest misbehaviors, reviewing what can go wrong is a useful way to introduce the traps that occur with any form of discipline.

IA children will engage in some of the milder forms of misbehaviors because they generally are well behaved. But the HM child is another matter, and it is best not to use ignoring for any of their misbehaviors. Use the more potent methods to get them firmly under control.

In the next chapter we'll discuss time out as a technique designed to deal with IA and HM children. If followed correctly rapid changes will occur in your child and you can sigh with relief because you won't need Ritalin.

8

USING TIME
OUT CORRECTLY
FOR THE IA
OR HM CHILD

T ime out is extremely popular and is recommended in numerous books. You may be asking at this point, "Well, what's new here?" A lot! What you will learn in this chapter is an extremely rigorous application of time out. The steps you will learn are specifically designed for IA or HM (ADD or ADHD) children to train them to think ahead, which means they will have to learn to remember at all times that their behavior will have consequences.

Traditional practices of time out fail with IA and HM children. You probably already know that. Follow the steps taught here and watch the remarkable results.

WHAT IS TIME OUT?

Calling *time out* means removing the misbehaving child from *all* material and social reinforcement and from all negative attention. When in time out, the child gets little or zero stimulation. In other words, it is completely boring. Children dislike time out more than spanking. My adult daughter, Heidi, reminiscing with me one day said, "Dad, when I was a kid I hated time out. I'd rather you'd spanked me than sent me to time out!"

I replied, "That was the whole idea." We both laughed. It is the most effective form of discipline I know and has none of the usual drawbacks we discussed earlier about punishment—physical contact or pain, the adaptation effect, or side effects such as anxiety or nervousness.

Our goals are to have the child develop a good sense of what is right or wrong, to pay attention to what she is doing at all times, and to think ahead of time about how she should behave. We will be using time out not just to control a behavior but to focus on the cognitive components of thinking and paying attention.

Time out can begin at age three, although I have used it on younger children.

This chapter explains how to use time out correctly in the home. Psychological research on time out offers a wide variety of methods, but what I present here is very rigorously designed and researched specifically for IA and HM children.

TIME OUT RULES FOR
THE IA OR HM CHILD

The following rules are designed to teach IA and HM youngsters to think and focus on their problematic patterns of behavior. *The more problematic a child's behavior, the more carefully we must apply our tools* to bring specific, identified target behaviors under control. Once your child is brought under control, the need to use time out will lessen considerably, and the majority of your interactions will be positive. You will also enjoy the benefits of taking your child to many places and feeling confident of his good behavior.

Use Time Out for Even a Hint of a Misbehavior

Identify each and every target behavior that is problematic. Being comprehensive is essential for the Caregivers' Skills Program to succeed. Begin with even a hint of a target behavior. For example, if you told Johnny to pick up his toys and he begins to turn away from his toys, say, "Go to time out!" If Joanne has a target behavior of talking back to you (defiance) and she merely looks at you in a glaring manner, immediately say, "Go to time out!" This may seem unduly tough, but with IA and HM children the CSP is designed to allow no quarter. It is designed for them to learn that they'd better pay careful attention to their behavior and not show the slightest sign of a misbehavior. This is a far better alternative than putting them on Ritalin or any other amphetamine. After four or five months of this extreme rigor, their behavior should be controlled well enough that you can lighten up a bit. But if you notice the target behavior returning, tighten up again for another four months.

Remember, one of the most important differences between the CSP and other programs is that we discipline at a hint of misbehavior—*before* the child loses control.

Choose a Suitable Environment

The environment for time out is very important. Designate a large, comfortable, overstuffed chair for time out and move it away from windows. Because children have active imaginations and can fantasize, looking out a window can be stimulating and therefore reinforce the target behavior.

Do not turn the chair to face the wall. That is humiliating—something we don't want. And don't place the chair where people can stare at the child because that can also be degrading and humiliating.

One father painted a dot on the wall and required his child to put his nose on the dot and stand there for time out. The placement of the dot forced the child to stand on tiptoe and caused his leg muscles to cramp. That was humiliating and abusive. When I found out what the father had done, I was furious and threatened to report him to the authorities unless he stopped immediately. *No discipline should ever embarrass, degrade, or torment a child.* For that same reason, do not use a hard wooden chair.

Situate the time out chair in a well-lighted place. Darkness fosters daydreaming and fantasizing in some children, which actually can be reinforcing. Also, some children might develop a fear of the dark, while others may doze off. Once they fall asleep, discipline is over.

The chair is best placed in a lightly trafficked area, so you can observe your youngster periodically to make sure she is all right, not getting out of the chair, and not doing something inappropriate, such as playing.

A heavily trafficked area may provide too much stimulation and may therefore be entertaining and reinforcing. In an area without traffic where youngsters can hear the observer coming, they will quickly sit up and behave. You will not be able to catch them doing anything wrong.

A child's bedroom has too many things that can distract, reinforce, or stimulate active fantasizing. It is only useful for time out if all these things are removed.

I have found that the ideal place for a time out chair is in a formal living room. Even if your house or apartment does not have a formal living room, I am confident you'll find a suitable location. *Your goal is to make the area around the chair as boring as possible.* Sit in the chair and pretend to be your youngster. What can you find to amuse yourself? Remove it!

Never use a bathroom for time out. Bathrooms are havens for things to play with, including things that can be dangerous.

Avoid Reinforcers Near the Time Out Chair

Competing reinforcers can neutralize the effectiveness of time out. A *competing reinforcer* is any object that can be played with. Clear the area near the chair of props your child may use for play or fantasy. Coasters or ashtrays can become flying saucers, paper can be folded into airplanes, pens can be rocket ships. By the way, I learned the hard way to empty my child's pockets of playthings before time out begins, which is especially important for little boys.

Another competing reinforcer may be a television the child can watch from a distance. I recall one case when time out did not seem to be working for seven-year-old Eric. When his parents sat in the chair and pretended to be their son, they realized that by leaning to the left they could watch a television at the end of a long hallway. Simply moving the chair a couple of feet to the right solved that problem easily.

Use Time Out Everywhere

Time out should be used in all situations and under all circumstances. This is essential if the parent is to help the child extend the good behaviors beyond the home environment. If children are disciplined only at home, they will learn to be well behaved only in the home. I assume that all parents want to be able to take their children anywhere—church, shopping, restaurants—and not be afraid the children will be disruptive.

To use time out away from home, simply designate a convenient place such as a bench in a mall, an empty table at a restaurant, or a corner of a grocery store; then ask your child to come to you. Firmly whisper in his ear to go to time out. Try to do this away from observers. If you embarrass your child, you may get a misbehavior under control but risk psychological and emotional scarring. If no separate place appears safe or available, you can use the back seat of your car except in bad or hot weather. For safety's sake, keep your child under careful observation at all times.

Choose the Right Amount of Time

You want your child to lose all sense of time, so scout around for clocks visible from the time out chair and remove them. Sitting in a chair even for a short time without being able to keep track of how much time has elapsed can seem like an eternity. If you doubt that, I suggest you sit in a chair for ten minutes. Don't look at your wristwatch; have another adult keep track of the time for you.

Those ten minutes will be the longest of your life. Imagine what it must be like for a seven- or eight-year-old with a highly charged, energetic body.

You, however, must keep careful track of time. A phone call or unexpected visitor can steal your attention and cause you to forget that your child is in the time out chair. Some parents have confessed to me that they accidentally left their youngster in the chair for three or more hours. To be honest with you, I have done this a few times myself. One teacher sent her recalcitrant charge to the school's time out room at nine o'clock and at two o'clock remembered he was still there. She hurried to the room and flung open the door. The child just stared at her in disbelief.

Please get a timer with a signal loud enough to alert you but not to be audible to your child in the chair. If your little one can hear it, she is warned to stop any misbehavior and sit up correctly for your approach. We want the child behaving in the chair for the full time, not only at the end at the sound of a timer. I also suggest a device you can carry with you in the event your child deserves time out outside the home. I use an inexpensive wristwatch with a stopwatch feature.

How long should children be in time out? Research indicates many lengths of time are effective. The figures I offer here are based on my years of experience.

Age	Minimum Time
3 to 4	3 minutes
4 to 5	5 minutes
5 to 11	10 minutes

Remember that these are minimum times. Do not let children out earlier.

Is there a maximum time in time out? Ideally, children should stay in time out until their behavior is perfect—sitting up and being completely quiet, no matter how long it takes. But if their behavior is perfect at the minimum time, they may come out.

If they are whining, pleading, kicking, humming, or whistling, they stay in time out until their behavior is perfect. If the child slowly and carefully slides down in the chair, his bottom is considered out of the seat. If he stands, his bottom is considered out of the seat. He does not then get to leave time out.

If children misbehave in time out, do not let them out while acting up, even if the time limit has been reached. That reinforces the misbehavior. Instead, when they finally sit up and behave, time one extra minute of quiet and then let them out. For example, if they misbehave for seventeen minutes and then finally sit up quietly, clock one minute of perfect behavior and then let them out. It is crucial for the IA or HM child that you follow these instructions precisely.

My records indicate that for children ages five to eleven, the average time for the first day is about nineteen to twenty minutes. Within three days, almost every child behaves within the minimum time. In my years of practice I have had four cases in which, on the first day, the children—severe IA or HM cases—stayed in for four hours. I was not surprised, because the parents' history of extreme inconsistency had trained the children to test their limits.

Do Not Talk to Your Child While in Time Out

Never talk to your child while he or she is in time out. Do not say, "If you stop crying, I'll let you out." Any interaction reinforces whatever misbehavior is going on at that moment in time out. Any dialogue prolongs the time you will need to get results. If you wish to discuss anything with your child, wait until he is involved in a quiet activity. The methods in this book do not preclude or interfere with talking to your children about behaviors and expectations, but do it when they are behaving well, not during a time out.

Never Physically Put a Child in Time Out

Avoid physically putting children into time out or physically taking them out, the only exception being if your child refuses to go to time out. Otherwise, youngsters must go in and come out on voice command. Physically putting your child in the chair can reinforce the very target behavior you are trying to extinguish.

If your child refuses to go to time out, you must have a sterner back-up procedure. Spanking is out. So you'll have to resort to putting him in physically. If the child, however, consistently refuses to go to time out, do this: Remove all reinforcing objects from his room. I know this is an inconvenience but it is essential. Put a lock on the outside of his door. Install a one-way peep-hole to allow you to check on his safety. He then has a choice—either go to the time out chair or go to the room. If he refuses to go to the chair, physically put him in his room, lock the door, and follow all the same procedures as you would when using the chair.

I know this may sound horrible to some readers. But the parent must establish who is the boss. *And allowing the IA or HM patterns of behavior to continue and putting a child on Ritalin is much worse for the child.* Usually the mere threat of having to go to the locked room is enough to persuade a child to go to time out.

Sometimes a child in the room will get wild and have a terrible temper tantrum. Don't be dismayed. I've had parents report this on a few occasions, but within a few days the tantrums not only stop but the child readily goes to the chair.

Deal with "I Need to Go to the Bathroom"

What if your child is commanded to go to time out and replies, "I need to go to the bathroom"? If the child is younger than five, let him go to the bathroom, then go back to time out. Children five and over can hold it for eight hours at night so they can certainly wait another ten minutes until the time out is completed. If a child over the age of five has an accident while in time out, he must clean up the mess. Once he finishes cleaning up, send him back to time out and start the ten minutes over. I doubt there will ever be another accident.

Insist that the Child Remember the Misbehavior

When children come out of time out, *they are required to tell you what they did wrong.* Ask them, "Why did you go to time out?" The burden of remembering is theirs (this is crucial for the IA or HM child), so do not remind them. After they tell you, then command them to do what they were supposed to do. Unless they comply *immediately,* they go back to time out and the time starts from zero.

They also return to time out if they can't remember what they did wrong. Begin the timing from zero. When the youngsters emerge, ask again, "Why did you go to time out?" You will be amazed by how rapidly their memory improves after the second time out. A crucial part of the CSP is that we train children to think, that is, to remember what they did wrong.

Many times I have witnessed Academy-Award-winning performances in which a child feigns an inability to remember what he did wrong. Don't buy it. Be strict. This is crucial in retraining the IA or HM child.

One couple I worked with called their daughter (whose real name was Melanie) Theda Bara—the name of a silent-screen movie actress. They said when she came out of time out and was asked what she did wrong, she'd screw her face up in several different expressions that conveyed utter confusion. When sent back to time out, she could always clearly explain what she did wrong in the first place. Within the first week she learned to tell after the first time out trial. When her parents first followed this procedure, the Dad said, "Why that little imp knew what she was doing all along."

Repeat no more than three times, however. If they still cannot tell you, then they are really confused. Simply tell them what they did and require the correct behavior.

For three- and four-year-olds, I am less strict. If they cannot respond, it's all right for you to tell them. But after age four, they *must* assume the responsibility for remembering what they did to be sent to the time out chair. Remembering requires them to think; you are now training them to fire their brain cells. When you begin to get them remembering what they should do, you too will stop believing the disease theories about ADD and ADHD and that Ritalin was necessary. You'll find that, indeed, when properly motivated with rigorous contingencies, children can function quite well.

Respond to Misbehaving on the Way to Time Out

What should you do if your child misbehaves on the way to time out by stomping a foot on the floor, kicking a chair, or cursing under her breath? When time is up, ask why she went in the first place. If the answer is correct, ask a second question: "What did you do on the way to time out?" Usually you will see a face covered with guilt. Tell your child to go back to time out for the *full* time.

Then ask, "Why did you have to go to time out a second time?" Once again she *must* tell you what she did wrong and then perform the behavior she was supposed to have done in the first place.

Reinforce Correct Behavior

No form of discipline will work if the parent does not reinforce correct behavior(s). Time out will reduce inappropriate behavior, but it will not teach the child new correct behaviors. Reinforcement—especially social reinforcement—will teach the child correct and appropriate behaviors.

As a result, I have been adding something new with my sons. When they come out of time out and tell me what they did wrong, I say, "Now give Daddy a kiss, and do what you're supposed to do." In this way they learn that I judge their behavior to be wrong but in no way have they lost my love.

Be Tough Consistently—Allow No Testing

Each and every inappropriate behavior, even an approximation of an incorrect response, should be met with time out. Don't let some target behaviors go past you while using time out for others. Inconsistency confuses the IA or HM child. If you err, err on the side of toughness. A good rule is "When in doubt, use time out." This is another crucial point of the CSP in working with IA and HM children.

Children will test you, and if you fail to use time out consistently, you'll be training them to test your limits constantly. This is the exact pattern of IA and HM children. I call them professional testers. If you allow testing behaviors, your child will become confused and won't learn the boundaries of his behaviors; you'll just prolong the time necessary to get him under control. You will also extend the need to discipline your youngster, and that is not fair. Inconsistency and hesitation do the child no favors.

Don't Bargain

Do not negotiate with your child. Once you have issued the command to go to time out, you should expect it to be followed immediately. Do not listen to the plea, "All right, Mommy, I'll pick up my toys," and back down. Any surrender on your part trains your sons and daughters to test behavior limits, that is, how far they can go with you and how badly they can misbehave. Always remember that the sooner you get results, the sooner your interactions with your child will be positive and reinforcing and, in turn, the sooner your child will be happier. This is the kindest thing you can do for the child. Bargaining is one of the biggest mistakes parents make. If an IA or HM child learns to bargain with you, he will not find it necessary to think preventively, that is, ahead of time.

Forcing the child to behave properly also moves him to the positive side of the triangle (see Figure 3.1 in Chapter Three), where he gets the praise he needs so desperately. *You do not help the IA or HM child by being weak.*

For years psychology and psychiatry have made us afraid to be strict. We fear we might psychologically scar a child. Remember that being strict does not mean being punitive. Keep in mind that once misbehaviors are brought under control, the primary and predominant interactions between you and your child will be positive and reinforcing. This is what IA and HM children need. Bargaining is not being strict with your child. Bargaining merely perpetuates their pattern, which is not helpful at all.

Be Consistent with the Other Parent

Whichever parent is with the child at the time of a misbehavior should use time out. There should not be any, "Wait 'til your father gets home!" This makes Mom look ineffective and Dad seem like the bad guy. If Mom fails to be consistent, then the child learns to misbehave with her—the weaker parent. Then Dad does not understand when Mom reports how bad the child has been with her, because the child is so well behaved when he is present. Sound familiar?

Respond Early and Quickly

Some behaviors begin with what we call preparatory behaviors— the child will do something mild and get progressively worse until finally he reaches a severe target behavior. For example, rarely does the child begin with a temper tantrum. Usually he begins with not listening to you—noncompliance. Then he talks back to you— oppositionalism. Then the tantrum comes. Put him in time out as soon as the noncompliance occurs. It is important that you intervene during the preparatory actions while the responses are mild rather than wait until the misbehavior is at its peak. Again, this is a key feature of the CSP.

Offer No Warnings

Other authors may disagree with me about this issue, but I stand firm on the importance of not giving warnings as reminders. Warning trains the child to not think. He doesn't have to attend to his own behavior. The child becomes reliant on the parent to remind him to behave, when actually the child should do the remembering. When you provide no warning, the child must constantly be aware of his ongoing behaviors if the consequences are to be avoided.

The technique of counting "one, two, three" is a warning. This reminds the child to pay attention. All youngsters, especially IA and HM children, must remember on their own what they are to do. Yes, when you warn or correct they will comply with the correct behavior, but five minutes later they will resume their "not thinking" pattern, which is exactly what we are combating. Getting them to think is crucial. It is not compliance with warnings that we are targeting with IA and HM children but remembering and paying attention to their own actions. That is the core of the CSP.

Sending the child to time out immediately, with no warning and no counting, is probably the most important rule to follow in the correct use of time out. Do it at all times. *Make them remember!*

Treat Siblings Equally

When your children's interactions get out of hand, send both of them to time out in different locations. Remember, when a sibling fight occurs as a target behavior, don't ask what is going on or who started it. Usually the innocent-looking one started it and the other child had the misfortune of getting caught. The odds are that both children amply contributed to the strife, so don't worry about punishing an innocent bystander.

Explain Time Out to Your Child

You want to prepare your child for time out to lessen confusion about the system. Explain time out only on two occasions: the night before you start and the night after you start. Never explain it again; experience will teach it well enough. You want your child to remember the rules. When you finish explaining, ask your child to explain it back to you. Clear up any misconceptions.

Do not become dismayed by his immediate reactions to your explanation. Some children cry, some laugh, and some shrug as if they could not possibly care less. No matter how children react to your explanation, they will soon learn to hate time out.

Keep the explanation simple. Don't review each target behavior. Otherwise, if you forget one or two you may hear: "But you didn't say that." Simply tell your child that he will go to time out for any and all misbehaviors and will stay in for exactly ten minutes (or the minimum time mentioned earlier) if behavior is perfect while in the chair. Explain that if he misbehaves while in time out, he will stay in until his behavior is proper and quiet.

Tell your children that they must think about what they did wrong whenever they go to time out and that they must tell you what it was when they come out. Say, "If you can't remember what you did wrong, then you will have to go back until you do remember." Do this only when explaining time out. Do not repeat this for each incident.

After the initial explanation, don't tell them to think about what they did wrong each time you use time out. Do not "remind them to remember." From the moment the rule is explained, they will be required to remember or face the consequences. This aspect is crucial for IA or HM children. Warn them about the locked room if and when they fail to go immediately to time out.

SOME THINGS THAT MAY GO WRONG

Here are some common occurrences parents have brought to my attention.

1. Your child may start to resume old habits. If so, you are probably being lax by not reinforcing enough or letting testing behaviors slip past you. Stay alert for warning signs that your child is starting to test you. Expect testing.

2. Spontaneous reappearance of target behaviors is likely. Don't become dismayed. Remember the rules for ignoring apply here, too (see Chapter Seven). Simply enforce the time out rules, and the testing will disappear quickly.

3. Matters *will* get worse before they get better. Because time out removes both social and material reinforcers, target behaviors will get worse and new misbehaviors, or new testing behaviors, will emerge. This generally gets rough for three or four days. Again, remember the graph we reviewed in the discussion of ignoring? It applies here, too. If you hang on, you will see dramatic improvement by the fourth or fifth day *without resorting to putting Ritalin in children's bodies.*

4. Most important of all, the key to success is love—social reinforcement for behaving correctly.

When my son Alex was seven years old, he threw a toy at Kevin, who was then five. Immediately Alex walked away, and I said, "Where are you going, Alex?" He replied, "To put myself in time out." How's that for training?

9

REINFORCEMENT REMOVAL FOR VERY DIFFICULT BEHAVIORS

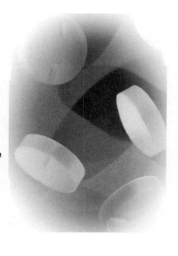

Even though the Caregivers' Skills Program is highly effective, some target behaviors may resist change. Two of the most resistant behaviors are aggression and lying. To deal with these tenacious behaviors, a powerful technique called reinforcement removal (RR) was developed.

If RR is added to the CSP, even these difficult behaviors can be quickly brought under control.

REINFORCEMENT REMOVAL

Reinforcement removal is the technique of taking away material reinforcers for a long period of time. For younger children the loss may be a week; for older children the loss is for longer periods of time—a month or even a year. For example, Alison has been told that her favorite doll will be taken away for a month if she tells a lie again. Her mother notices Alison playing outside with her brother and beginning to argue with him over who's to play with the ball. Billy grabs it from her hands and Alison runs in the house yelling, "Billy hit me."

The correct response is, "Alison, you just lied. I was watching and Billy took the ball away from you, which is his in the first place. He didn't hit you. You know the consequences. Please bring me your doll now. How long did I tell you you'd lose it?" It is a powerful technique that should be reserved for more difficult behavior problems, such as Alison's lying.

Using RR Correctly

Time periods that work best for RR depend on age: a week for three- and four-year-olds, a month for five- to seven-year-olds, and a year above the age of eight. It must be used precisely. The pattern of behavior that will occur following this loss is similar to ignoring, that is, the target behavior will get worse, new target behaviors will appear, and eventually the target behavior will return for a brief period. RR is an extremely strong approach and for that reason is best reserved for times when everything else has failed. Here's how to implement RR.

Make a list of at least seven objects and activities that are most important to your son or daughter. Examples are using the telephone to talk to friends, riding a bicycle, playing video games, listening to favorite CD's, watching a favorite TV show, going to the movies, or going camping. Do not choose things that are impractical to take away, such as reading. Prioritize the list, with number 1 being the most important to the child and number 7 being very important but the least important on the list. Remember, if an item is not important to the child, this won't work.

Explain to the child that if he engages in a serious act such as aggression, he will lose an item for a long period of time. For example, "Ricky, if you hit your sister, or anyone, you'll lose your bicycle for a month. If you do it again remember the next items on our list." Many parents feel this may be too strict, but remember a behavior such as aggression is so dangerous that it calls for strong measures.

I have also used this method successfully with aggressive teenagers—some referred to me by the police because their aggression had reached very dangerous levels.

Begin with the loss of item 7 and for each act move up the list. Each aggressive act serves as an increasingly uncomfortable loss. Keep a record for yourself of the starting date as a reminder. This method has worked overwhelmingly well, even with extremely difficult cases—Greg, for example, whom we'll meet shortly.

It's also important to have a backup if your child uses an item while it is confiscated. The back-up must be particularly strong and thus very meaningful. Two methods that work well are (1) to be permitted no contact with friends for a week and (2) to give away or sell the item. Use this only after the first method has failed two times, and warn your child ahead of time that this will be the consequence.

Example: Greg

Greg was an eleven-year-old whose mother came to my office feeling extremely guilty and desperate. She loved her child, but at the same time she "hated" him. Her boyfriend had also tried, in vain, to control the child.

Greg's mother was struggling financially, working extremely hard as a janitor, raising two younger children, trying to spend time with her boyfriend, and dealing with an HM-aggressive child. The stress was taking its toll on her.

We followed the Caregivers' Skills Program and in less than two months, without medication, brought all target behaviors under control except aggression. On a daily basis Greg's behaviors at home improved. He readily did as he was told, his poor me's and whining stopped, he no longer nagged, and he stopped interrupting his mother's conversations. And his schoolwork improved. He paid attention in class, completed all his work, stopped acting like the class clown, and was polite to his teacher.

However, Greg continued to lose his temper on rare occasions. My research with some cases of IA and HM children indicates that this pattern of controlling all behaviors *except* aggression does happen. There are several reasons for this. Other target behaviors occur frequently, allowing lots of chances for training new behaviors. Aggression typically occurs only on rare occasions, thus allowing few opportunities for training. In addition, loss of temper and violent rage are such powerful emotions that they are more difficult for a child to contain. This is why these stronger techniques are needed. Aggression is actually very resistant to almost all forms of traditional treatment, which is why I developed and researched the use of RR to deal with it.

Greg's aggression occurred only about twice a month. He would use his fist to hit other children or even his mother, sometimes with an object in his hand. Once he broke a pool cue over another boy's head.

Reasoning with Greg about his aggressiveness failed. He promised repeatedly to do better but did not. Promises to behave better with aggressive IA or HM children are quite common, and indeed I believe children are sincere when they promise. However, for the reasons just given, they often don't succeed and need the help of RR to add more incentive. With Greg we then started the RR program. Each aggressive act meant the loss of an item for one year; dates were recorded in a notebook. His mother listed the following seven items:

1. Dungeons and Dragons game
2. Guitar playing
3. Watching television
4. Riding his bicycle
5. Calling his friends
6. Going to the movies
7. Eating Mallomars

If he was found using an item when it had been taken away, he would then not be permitted contact with his friends for one week. This is a strong backup technique.

I knew this would be a difficult case because Greg's mother had a history of inconsistency. Greg expected his mother not to follow through with her threats. (Her inconsistency had already bred persistency.)

The aggression persisted through the first six items. His mother managed to carry out the contingencies to the letter. Finally, at item 1, the aggression halted. I sighed with relief. Most children stop the aggression after the loss of three items.

Several weeks later in a follow-up session, Greg was crying happy tears in my office. His mother's boyfriend had bought him an expensive pocketknife as a gift, and they had started going fishing together. Greg had never been treated this way. I cried in that session, too.

Generally, for children below the age of five, I have found that the CSP—the combination and judicious use of time out and social reinforcement—control aggression extremely well. From the age of five through age twelve, the CSP alone works less well for aggression; RR may have to be added at that point.

Whether the method of discipline is ignoring, time out, or RR, don't forget to actively reinforce your child when he is behaving well. Are you getting sick and tired of my repeating this? If you want to keep your IA or HM child away from Ritalin, I can't emphasize this point enough. Discipline suppresses the target behaviors, but learning new and more appropriate behaviors requires very active social reinforcement. Be a bona fide hugger and kisser.

10

IMPROVING SCHOOL PERFORMANCE

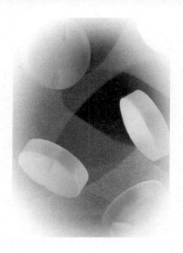

Congratulations! Your home life is much easier and more peaceful and loving now. So are you ready to take on your youngster's school performance? Then let's begin!

I'm devoting a separate chapter to improving school performance because it is one of the most frequent problems with IA and HM children. Children who act out to an extreme and who fail to behave at home do so at school, and vice versa. The good news is that in approximately 80 to 90 percent of my cases, once the behaviors at home are brought under control, school performance improves automatically. Please do not use the methods in this chapter until your child's target behaviors are under control at home. Until that time, set this book aside and practice the reinforcement described in the earlier chapters.

Your child may have already begun to settle down in the classroom. The quality and quantity of loving attention in a reinforcing home will help motivate children to perform better in outside settings. But if your child continues to do poorly in school once target behaviors are well under control at home, you will find this chapter especially helpful because it addresses this issue.

DEVELOP A PROGRAM

Let's begin with this ground rule: *The key to improved school performance is your child's motivation.* Highly motivated children come from families that consistently pay attention to their children's schoolwork and consistently reinforce them for their hard efforts. All of us are what we believe. If children are carefully nurtured early in life to love their education, to read and treasure books, and to work hard, they probably will develop the motivation to perform well in school. Behavioral programs and pills like Ritalin will not be necessary in the first place.

Remember our discussion about stress and how busy our lives are. We must carve out time each day to gently and lovingly instill positive values and beliefs. This motivation evolves from love, caring, nurturance, and attention in the home. Highly motivated youngsters will learn without fancy classroom equipment; all they need are the bare essentials: books, paper, pencils, and blackboards. And let's stop blaming the teachers. Even with the finest teachers and the best equipment, unmotivated children will not learn.

With the CSP, once behavior at home has settled down, you can work on nurturing the values that underlie and motivate good school performance. If your child is in the 20 percent for whom school performance did not improve, the following program can be implemented.

THINGS TO CHECK BEFORE BEGINNING THE PROGRAM

When a family brings a youngster to my office due to poor school performance, usually the child has been diagnosed as ADD or ADHD. In fact, almost every child sent to me these days comes with such a diagnosis. Consequently, I must consider four things:

1. *Has the child been tested for learning disabilities?* I have had many patients whose learning disabilities went undetected in schools for many years. Learning disabilities markedly impair academic performance. Have your child tested.

2. *Is anyone terrorizing the child?* Is he the victim of a school bully? Similarly, is the child's teacher overly negative, intimidating, or punitive? I recall one case in which a child's performance improved both at home and at school with the CSP. But every few weeks the gains would collapse. I asked to have a conference with his teacher and found the woman to be very harsh. The little boy finally admitted to me that this teacher scared him.

I tried to explain to the teacher the impact her approach was having on my patient, but she believed in her ways and would not change. Furthermore, she justified the rightness of her stance because her husband was a psychologist. (I told her that my ex-wife was a dentist. Did that mean she would she like me to perform a root canal on her?) The child transferred to a new class with a very positive teacher. His performance improved immediately, and no problems have emerged since.

3. *What is the child's readiness quotient (RQ)?* I usually assess the child's RQ—a term I prefer to IQ (intelligence quotient)—as well as skills in other subjects, such as reading and math. I prefer RQ to IQ because IQ is misleading. The purpose of Alfred Binet's so-called intelligence test, which he developed before the turn of the century, was actually to assess a child's readiness for school, even though the term *intelligence* has become attached to it. In fact, the written test does not reflect a child's intelligence. This can be confirmed by noting that many people who do not have high academic skills are extremely bright. But they probably would not do well on these tests.

Those arguments aside, psychologists often administer tests that yield a score called the IQ or intelligence quotient, which compares a child with other children in his or her age group. A number of 100 is right in the middle, that is, 90–110 is considered an average level of intelligence. Numbers above this level are associated with children who should be able to perform well in school, and numbers below represent the slower learners; the numbers drop all the way to the lower levels of retardation.

If a child's readiness is below grade level, the academic curriculum may be too difficult; a slow learner may not be able to compete with peers. The inability to keep up may underlie a pattern of being IA or HM. Under these circumstances the child may need to be placed in a self-paced class or in a class with fewer students where she can get individual attention. These classes often do not use traditional grading methods. Instead, the child is assessed by whether or not she is making consistent progress.

A child with a high RQ may be bored and insufficiently stimulated, and this too can underlie inattentiveness and misbehavior.

4. *Have your child's vision and hearing examined by a doctor.* Sometimes a subtle problem may have gone undetected.

If educational tests, RQ (IQ) tests, LD tests, and hearing and vision are all in normal range, we can conclude that no problems are present and that the child is bright enough to perform well. More direct intervention can begin. If you've successfully carried out the CSP at home and your child is well behaved, your child is a bit more stubborn than most and needs some additional work to get more improvement in the classroom. The following daily report card program is, therefore, added to the CSP to help with this problem.

A DAILY REPORT CARD

In most locales report cards are given every six weeks. This time span is of little help in shaping academic performance, which requires frequent, immediate, and consistent reinforcement for good performance. You and your child need to know each day how the child is doing in school. A daily sheet or report card, which is shown in Figure 10.1 and which you have permission to copy and use, gives sufficient feedback, allows your child to have a fresh start

Figure 10.1. Daily Report Card.

NAME: _____

DATE: _____

Subjects	CLASS PERFORMANCE (Doing work, Participation and attention)				CONDUCT IN CLASS				TESTS AND QUIZ GRADES (Returned Today)	HOMEWORK GRADES (Returned Today)	TEACHER'S INITIALS
	E	S	N	U	E	S	N	U			
1.											
2.											
3.											
4.											
5.											
6.											
7.											
8.											
9.											
10.											
11.											
12.											

COMMENTS: _____

_____

_____

_____

E = Excellent
S = Satisfactory
N = Needs Improvement
U = Unsatisfactory

every morning, and helps your youngster understand what areas
need to improve. This report card is used to coordinate your and
your child's teacher's efforts to help your child perform better.

The first order of business is to meet with your child's teacher.
Discuss with her how this report card can help both your child *and
her*. Filling out the report card every day may be interpreted by the
teacher as an intrusion in an already busy schedule. Explain that
this report card will help make her life much easier, since your child
has been disrupting her class. Point out that you suspect this con-
sumes a considerable portion of her time in dealing with him and
probably contributes to both disturbing the entire class and upset-
ting her nerves. When she realizes that the report card will help you
carry out meaningful consequences at home, which will get your
child to settle down and make life in the classroom considerably
more peaceful, I suspect she'll readily help. Most teachers want very
much to help a child who is having difficulty and are thrilled when
a parent wants to do something about it. I've rarely had a teacher
refuse to help, once the benefits were made clear.

Sometimes a teacher may say she can't do this for twenty-five
children. In fact, the method is only needed for one or two IA and
HM children. It is certainly worth the teacher's brief time and
effort to help these children and get them under control. However, if the teacher does refuse to help, I urge you to speak with
the principal. In my experience, the principal will, without exception, direct the teacher to assist a child who has been failing for a
very long time. It might be useful to offer to let the teacher read
your copy of this book. This is the easiest way to clarify what our
goals are.

Often, IA and HM children are not aware that their performance is poor. Many students believe they are doing well because
they performed well on the last two or three quizzes and seem to forget the failing grades of a couple of weeks before. This is extremely
common. Begin by giving your youngster the responsibility to record
all test grades (Figure 10.2). Have your child post the scores in a

Figure 10.2 Record of Test Grades to Be Posted at Home.

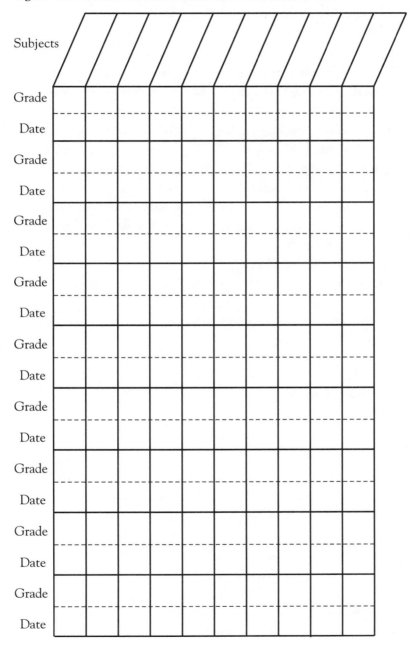

convenient location as a constant visual reminder of his standing at any given time.

The daily report card (Figure 10.1) can enhance communication between you and the teacher, who, if she has agreed, can complete the daily assessment in only a few minutes. Your son or daughter returns the form to you each day. *This report card is essential because you control the daily consequences at home.*

In column 1, subjects are listed in the order they are scheduled for the day. All aspects of the child's performance are then evaluated for each subject.

In column 2, we assess Class Performance, which is the teacher's estimate of how well the child is paying attention in class and how well he is participating in class discussion. The grade is a collective estimate made by the teacher on behaviors such as the child carefully doing his work and staying on task, listening carefully, looking at the board or the teacher, and participating in class discussions and answering questions. The behaviors in this category include all the behaviors listed in the *DSM-IV* for attention problems. The following grades represent the teacher's estimate:

E = Excellent

S = Satisfactory

N = Needs Improvement

U = Unsatisfactory

Giving a single grade makes communication much easier for the teacher. Listing every detail is too time consuming and impractical, and may even lose the teacher's cooperation.

Column 3 (Conduct) includes inappropriate behaviors such as talking to another student during work time, walking around without permission, excessive fidgeting, calling out in class, pushing in line, and so forth. In the *DSM-IV* these are listed as impulse control problems. Conduct is assessed collectively for all problem behaviors; the teacher checks the appropriate column each day.

Test and Quiz Grades are recorded in column 4. Homework Grades are also recorded by the teacher in column 5. Sometimes teachers grade this A, B, C, D, and F, and sometimes a numerical score is given. Be sure to know the letter equivalents for the numerical scores because they differ in some school districts. For example, in some school systems an 84 is a B, but in others it is a C.

The final column is reserved for the teacher's initials.

At the end of the school quarter, the sheets should closely match the regular report-card grades. If you find an inconsistency between the report card and the daily reports, then the teacher may not be using the daily sheet correctly.

I encourage you to meet with the teacher every two weeks to review your child's progress until all the problems dramatically improve. Improvement means that your child is passing everything, that is, class performance is at S or better, conduct is at S or better, test and homework grades are at C or better. If your child passes everything, there should be positive consequences at home; if even one grade is failed, discipline should ensue at home, such as loss of free play.

Set Required Levels of Performance

In class participation, the teacher observes your child in class and estimates how well he is doing his work. Is he staying on task, participating in class discussion, raising his hand properly, and answering questions? This estimate is made during each subject throughout the day.

For conduct, the teacher reports her observations about how well your child is behaving. Is he talking to other children around him, calling out answers without raising his hand, getting out of his seat, pushing other children when in line, and walking around the room without permission? Again, this estimate is made for each subject throughout the day.

Criterion level refers to the minimum passing grade. An N or a U in either Class Participation or Conduct is considered a failure, that is, below criterion level. The minimum passing level is an S. One N (or U) in any subject means negative consequences at home, such as not being allowed free play.

For example, Matthew was a severe IA-HM child. In class he often stared out the window. He completed his work in a sloppy fashion, often not answering all the questions; he wouldn't answer the teacher's questions. As for conduct, he fidgeted in his seat, got out of his seat and walked around the room, and constantly talked to other children around him. His parents had successfully completed the CSP at home, but his schoolwork didn't improve. The daily report card program was begun. During the first week he did extremely poorly, necessitating his loss of free play from 3:30 to 5:00 P.M. each day. By the second week his grades were improving, and by Wednesday his report card looked like the one in Figure 10.3.

Notice that Matthew passed everything except for one grade in math, where he received an N for Conduct—one grade below criterion. That day he still lost free play. However, on Thursday he passed everything and was allowed his free play time. He's passed everything since.

Tests, Quizzes, and Homework

If an IA and HM child tests within the average range or higher during my initial assessment, we can expect grades on the daily sheet to be roughly in the C or B range. Thus the criterion level is C. If he tests high, then we can expect B's or A's; therefore the criterion is set at B.

If the child scores at or above criterion level, the child earns reinforcers at home. If the child performs below grade level *academically or behaviorally*, even if only one grade, one conduct mark, one test grade, or if one homework grade is below criterion level, then he experiences negative consequences at home.

"Only *one?*" you may ask. Yes. I have had numerous cases of children drastically failing in conduct, classwork, and homework, and within one week after beginning the grade sheet, their performances

Figure 10.3. Daily Report Card Sample.

NAME: _Matthew_

DATE: _4/12_

Subjects	CLASS PERFORMANCE (Doing work, Participation and attention)				CONDUCT IN CLASS				TESTS AND QUIZ GRADES (Returned Today)	HOMEWORK GRADES (Returned Today)	TEACHER'S INITIALS
	E	S	N	U	E	S	N	U			
1. Science		✓				✓			Quiz 85	92	J.T.
2. Reading	✓					✓			—	90	J.T.
3. Music	✓				✓				—	—	E. S.
4. Math		✓					✓		Quiz 83	90	J.T.
5. Phys. Ed.	✓				✓				—	—	B. W.
6. Lunch		✓				✓			—	—	J.T.
7. Language		✓			✓				Test 94	No Homework returned	J.T.
8. Art	✓								Completed Project 100	—	P. S.
9.											
10.											
11.											
12.											

COMMENTS: _Matthew did very well on his Language Test! During Math we talked with his friend while we were doing a practice exercise._

E = Excellent
S = Satisfactory
N = Needs Improvement
U = Unsatisfactory

improved to passing. Setting such strict standards forces the child to immediately perform at his best. It also communicates simply and clearly what we expect of the child, thus eliminating confusion or misunderstandings.

Can the IA and HM child really do this? Yes! Yes! Yes! I've been through this hundreds of times with hundreds of cases, and the answer is yes. They are not diseased. They are normal children who can do this.

Robert was an IA child. His conduct was always considered excellent. He was soft-spoken and rarely misbehaved. However, his class participation was consistently poor because he rarely paid attention, constantly looked around the room instead of looking at his work, and performed his work in a sloppy fashion. His home-work and test grades were almost always N's or U's. His RQ was 122 (quite high), he had no learning disabilities, and his hearing and vision were normal.

In the first week of the daily report card program, his class per-formance improved to passing and his tests and homework grades improved. However, on Monday of the second week he received a D in reading and a D in social studies. He also failed tests in math and social studies. He lost free play that day from 3:00 to 5:00 P.M. On Tuesday he passed everything except for one homework grade in math. Again he lost free play. On Wednesday he passed every-thing and was permitted free play. In the following three weeks, on two days he received one failing grade in different subjects. On those days he lost free play. In the weeks that followed he passed everything and, henceforth, was allowed free play every day.

WHAT ARE THE CONSEQUENCES?

Recall that reinforcers are objects (toys, candy) and activities (free play, TV time).

Michael loved watching cartoons after school each day. He had successfully improved in all home behaviors on the CSP, and his school performance had dramatically improved except for his homework, which was usually incomplete and done sloppily. For one week he continued to fail in homework for most of his subjects, which meant no cartoons and no substitutes, that is, he was not allowed to do anything else. By the second week he understood what was expected, and he began doing his homework neatly and carefully, thus passing each day in all subjects. He began watching his daily cartoons.

A negative consequence may be the loss of free play after school from 3:30 to 5:00 P.M. And no substitutions! No television, no reading, no telephone calls, no homework, no games, no visitors—nothing for two hours. *Remember the "no substitutions" rule for discipline.*

Unlike grounding for six weeks, each day is a new beginning. Youngsters can decide to perform well the next day or get the consequences again. Remember the daily rule. If children resist improving after a few weeks, we can add removing the hour allowed for watching television—also with no substitutions. If necessary, we can get even tougher, but frankly (and fortunately) this rarely happens.

On many occasions with children with high RQ scores, I immediately set the expectations for Test and Homework at all B's and A's. I have found that children who have the ability can indeed improve performance to that level, again in only one week.

Will scored an RQ of 144, which is enormously high. He was consistently getting D's and F's in all his subjects for tests and homework. Because of his RQ, criterion level was set at B. His parents felt this was somewhat strict but reluctantly agreed to try it. Will was told he couldn't ride his bicycle after school each day if he made below a B on either homework or tests. The mere mentioning of this was sufficient. On Monday he made two A's and the rest of his grades were B's. Will really liked all the praise and compliments he was getting from his teachers and parents. He seemed surprised that he could do so well. His self-esteem improved. By the second week he began making almost straight A's. He's been an honor student ever since.

Some parents I have known wanted to be more lenient and allow three C's for homework and tests rather than all B's and A's. I have found as a result that the child will get exactly three C's every day and usually not in the same subjects. Yes, children can discriminate that well.

If you wish, you can increase your expectations gradually each week to shape school performance gently and slowly. For example, you may set the second week's level at two C's, the third week at one C, and the fourth week at no C's. I prefer, however, setting stricter requirements at the start, as I did with Will.

Homework

Do not sit with children when they are doing homework. Let the consequences of the report card do the work. Do not reinforce children's helplessness. You may serve as a resource to answer questions, but do not sit with them and coach them. This is another major difference in the CSP. Trust that your child is normal and can do the work. Once you actually see these changes you will be a firm believer.

The two greatest lies are, "Mommy, the teacher never gives us any homework," and "Teacher, I lost it on the bus."

Homework is often a major issue, and parents with an IA and HM child generally force their youngster to do homework. I hear all the time, "If I don't sit with him, he won't do it." Remember that sitting with the child and prompting, coaxing, and cueing reinforces forgetfulness, task dependency, and "not thinking." Act only as a resource. When he finishes the work, check for neatness and accuracy. Point out what needs correction and then let your child struggle with it at his desk. The daily consequences for failing Homework on the report card will quickly get your child to improve as it did for Will.

Please remember: don't start the school program until your child's behaviors are extremely well controlled at home and you have allowed an additional few weeks to determine if the improvements transfer to improvement at school, in which case this school program is not needed.

The Blessed Snowball Effect

Once your child reaches grade-level performance, *intrinsic* (natural) reinforcement takes over, and the child enjoys discovering that he can perform at a higher level. This feels wonderful! Teachers tend to smile and treat the child better when improvement appears. Parents also tend to be more positive and reinforcing. These natural reinforcers help the child feel content and proud. They realize how good it feels to be "up there" academically.

Remember that a single grade below your expectation (criterion level) in any area—class performance, conduct, tests, or homework—means loss of privileges that day.

The daily report card determines what your child may or may not do after school that day. The child must remember the cause and effect of her actions in school without being reminded. Carry out the consequences calmly and efficiently.

You must stop yelling, screaming, pleading, and hitting to force your child to behave or do schoolwork. If you continue that pattern of punishment, your child will probably never improve. These methods do not work. Let the program work for you.

Most parents who use my approach will find that their child's grades and conduct improve and the child's nervousness subsides. With improvement in school comes an increase in intrinsic reinforcers, and parents frequently tell me that the child begins to appear much happier and much more at peace.

PREPARING TO BEGIN THIS PROGRAM

Review the program with the child before using it, then ask your youngster to explain the program to you. Clarify any confusions or misconceptions. Repeat this only one additional time. If the child still seems confused, simply go ahead and start the program. With

the process in operation your son or daughter will begin to understand in a very short time. Let's look at the case of Adam.

Adam was a nine-year-old in the fourth grade. His teacher, Mrs.
Johnson, requested that the parents seek professional help because
Adam was failing almost all his subjects. The teacher believed he was
bright and could do much better. His yearly national test scores indicated that his academic skills were considerably better than his
grades were reflecting.

Mrs. Johnson suggested that his parents discuss the use of
Ritalin with their family doctor. Adam was placed on Ritalin but no
improvements occurred. The school counselor in a conference with
his parents referred them to me.

An initial assessment indicated that Adam's reading and math
capabilities were a couple of years more advanced than his fourth-
grade placement. His full-scale RQ was 123; testing indicated that
he had no learning disabilities; the results of eye and ear examina-
tions were normal. He was clearly capable of doing much better
schoolwork. I requested that they discuss with their doctor the possibility of taking Adam off Ritalin. Under the doctor's supervision, the
Ritalin was gradually stopped.

Adam was not a severe behavioral problem in school, but Mrs.
Johnson observed that he would not stay on task and often seemed
bored. He talked to other children, interfered with their work, and
played with his pens and pencils as if they were rocket ships. Adam
was never rude; in fact he was considered a nice young man. The
school psychologist diagnosed Adam as ADD.

His parents indicated to me that Adam was a bit of a problem at
home. His misbehaviors included being noncompliant, oppositional,
and having one or two temper tantrums a week. He voiced poor-me
statements and negative verbalizations several times a day and
whined and cried, especially when he was supposed to be doing his
homework. His mother sat with him each evening while he did his

homework. If she was not with him, he would not do it. No other target behaviors were reported.

Adam's mother, a housewife, greeted him at home after school. He was allowed to play from 3:30 to 5:30 P.M. each day. After dinner Adam hastily worked on his homework, which was typically sloppy and often incomplete, then he watched television or read. Fortunately, Adam liked to read. Isn't it amazing how his so-called ADD disappeared when he was doing things he liked?

The family began parent training and after four sessions began the CSP. All target behaviors at home improved and Adam seemed more content, but the improvement did not extend to his schoolwork.

At my behest, Adam's parents took the daily report card to his teacher. Mrs. Johnson was eager to cooperate and Adam brought home reports each day. Adam understood that he would lose free play each day if his daily report cards showed any grade level below what was expected of him. This continued for one week. His home behaviors remained stabilized, but school performance improved only slightly. After the third week, not being allowed to watch television was added as a restriction. During the loss of free play and TV time, he was allowed only to walk around the house—no toys, no play, no homework, no reading, no cuddling with a family member (no substitutions). His class grades and homework then improved dramatically. Within three weeks he was achieving the required level of performance almost every day. His mother no longer sat with him when he did his homework; instead, she only served as a resource.

Within six weeks after his parents started the daily report card program, Adam was doing extremely well both in school and at home. He was more astonished than anyone else that he could perform so well in school. Mrs. Johnson went out of her way to reinforce his improvements. Visits to my office showed that Adam was a much happier child. His parents confirmed my observation. In a little more than three months this case was complete. Most cases are successful within two months.

THE VALUE OF
EDUCATION AND READING

To stabilize the gains you have made, it is essential that you work in a positive way to make reading and education important values to your child. Too many parents think their child should do well in school without reading and education being important family values. It doesn't work that way.

In families where these values are successfully instilled, the children do not become IA or HM. For children who are IA or HM, if you followed the CSP and the daily report card program, some of the behaviors and cognitive problems are probably under control. But it may not be enough. Your child may be well behaved and doing well in school, with natural reinforcers helping to change your child's attitudes. Teachers are smiling and praising more, you are reinforcing actively, your child is getting along well with other children— but there's still more to do. We have to further strengthen the values of education and reading.

Education

Earlier we discussed ways to make education and learning important, but perhaps it bears some repeating. Take your child on short educational trips. Visit museums, college campuses, and historical places. Make learning about nature important and fun. Take trips to scenic places. Go camping and teach your child camping skills. Go hiking. Get up early to watch the sun rise. Buy a telescope and scan the heavens. Instead of toys, buy microscopes, chemistry sets, or ant colonies and experiment with them with your child. Have your child help plant flowers and shrubs. Visit planetariums. Show an enthusiastic interest in your children's schoolwork. Talk with them every day about their day in school. Show your pleasure when they get a good grade.

Demonstrate your love for music. I love rock, pop, and classical music. Therefore, I take my children to the milder forms of rock concerts as well as to the symphony. I've found that kids often don't like classical music until they attend a live concert and then there is a positive attitude change.

Take your child to plays. Many communities have free outdoor presentations (also concerts) during the summer. Go as a family. I promise that you'll have fun, too.

Reading

I can't emphasize enough the importance of helping your child become a reader. Readers perform better than nonreaders in school and on national tests. Reading is so very important throughout life. To get children to become readers it is important to help them learn to love reading. To do this we have to make reading a fun activity, so here are ten helpful hints to make that happen.

1. *Read to your children and choose subjects of interest to them.* When you read to them, select materials that are at or above their current reading level (not grade level). Reading level is determined mostly by twice-yearly reading-skills tests; you should know these scores. Ask your child's teacher to explain the scores to you if you feel confused. Poor readers usually are below grade level in reading skills. Libraries and bookstores generally group books according to reading grade level.

When you read to them from more challenging books, you can expose them to more advanced vocabulary that will help with word-recognition skills and make it easier for them to decipher new words. Developmentally, children have excellent auditory learning skills that help with language learning. Be careful, though, to go no more than three grades above their current reading level. If younger children want the same book read to them each night, coax them to listen to something new, but if they don't want to, let it go. Better to keep the reading fun.

2. *When they read on their own, select material that is equal to or lower than their current reading level.* Reading is much more fun when a child doesn't trip over every other word. Let them get into

enjoying the content of the material. If they enjoy it, they'll do it. If they develop the reading habit, their reading skills will automatically improve.

3. *Allow children to read in bed for thirty minutes at bedtime*. Many children, especially HM children, do not want to go to sleep at bedtime. They'll love being given this extra time to stay up. If they ask to do anything else—draw or play with a toy, for example—your answer should be a flat no. Only reading is allowed. Younger prereaders can begin this nightly habit by looking at pictures. Remember, let children choose bedtime reading materials from their current and lower reading levels. Reading before bed or for pleasure should be easy and fun, not the chore that reading can be at school.

4. *Take trips to the library at least every other week*. Make these trips special. Visiting the library should become an activity that children anticipate with excitement. Teach them that the library should be a place they love. Let them choose books on subjects they like. Gently encourage them to explore new topics, but don't insist. Again, select reading material at relatively easy levels.

5. *Subscribe to children's magazines and newsletters*. Children are thrilled when the mail arrives bringing subscriptions in their name. Many magazines include fun exercises for children to do alone or with you.

6. *Allow comic books—they are perfectly fine*. Don't be persuaded by the myth that they hurt reading ability. If children enjoy them, comics can contribute to making reading a joy. Do, however, choose carefully. Some comics are risqué and violent. Look for those that are fun to read and appropriate to the child's age.

7. *During quiet periods with your children, ask them about their reading*. But do not push such conversations or pressure your child. If he seems excited and talks about the reading material, then listen and share the excitement.

8. *If you can afford to, buy books children can read and enjoy*. Build a library for them. Teach them to treat books with tenderness and love. Teach them that books are sacred treasures.

9. *Take time to read for your own enjoyment and set an example that will foster a love for the written word.* Shut off the television in the evening and sit and read as a family. During my household's nightly reading time, I have one son's head on my lap and the other boy snuggled on my shoulder. I love this, and I feel they do, too.

10. *Leave magazines around the house.* Choose them wisely so they are suitable for children.

Our goal is to see your child buried in a book sometime during each day and night of their lives. If at night you peek into your child's bedroom after he is supposed to be asleep and you see him reading with a flashlight under the cover, quietly back out and smile. You've succeeded.

IMPROVE SELF-ESTEEM EVEN MORE

Now that your child's school and home environments are improved, let's review how we can help improve self-esteem. The CSP and the daily report card program change children's surroundings from negative to positive: teachers like them more, other kids like them more, their grades are better, and all this helps. But in the next chapter let's review how to be certain your child is feeling even better about herself. Remember what the IA or HM child has been through in life—the disdain, the criticism, the punishment, and *Ritalin.* A new, positive self-image is so important. On to the next chapter.

11

HELPING THE IA
OR HM CHILD
TO FEEL BETTER

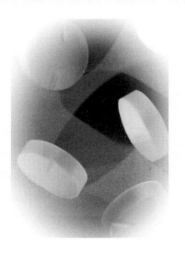

In this chapter we'll discuss additional ways to improve our children's self-worth. Typically, getting them under control with the Caregivers' Skills Program produces dramatic behavioral improvements; adults and peers then treat them more positively, which is crucial for positive self-esteem. However, parents can do some extra things to help IA or HM children feel even better and ensure that they won't ever need Ritalin again.

Removing overstimulation and having quiet time helps children feel more calm and at peace. Calming nervousness helps reduce the typical behavioral and cognitive problems. We'll review some suggestions for helping make this happen.

IMPROVING SELF-ESTEEM

How children feel about themselves is more crucial to their healthy development than any other factor. Their self-feelings are determined by thoughts, beliefs, and attitudes, as well as their deepest beliefs about themselves, which we call self-image or self-esteem.

Psychologist Eric Berne called this positive self-image "I'm OK." This chapter will explore the negative thought patterns and feelings—"I'm Not OK"—that are typical of IA or HM children and discuss how to change them.

A poor self-image almost guarantees a life of repeated failures and an ever-deepening loss of self-worth. This vicious cycle gets reinforced from almost every direction. Let's review how this occurs.

IA and HM children suffer from low self-esteem for three basic reasons.

1. They are impulsive and obnoxious in many ways, so they are often the butt of teasing and ridicule from other children. If their temper flares up as a reaction to this treatment, the ridicule worsens.

2. Parents and teachers sometimes call IA or HM children stupid and lazy. Fortunately, most teachers and parents try to avoid such cruelty. Keep in mind, however, that subtle looks of anger, disappointment, and scorn have a powerful effect on a child. Adults may not mean to do this; facial expressions and body language are natural reactions that are hard to mask but are devastating to the emotional development of these children.

3. The IA or HM child's self-deprecating, poor-me and negative statements are verbal habits that can become internalized and eventually become their true feelings and beliefs. When IA or HM children get their way or win attention or pity for these verbalizations, the adult reinforces them—however unintentionally. Each incident of reinforcement strengthens the verbal pattern into a habit. With constant repetition, youngsters lose the ability to discriminate between when they are feeling bad and when they are manipulating, so over time they increasingly do feel bad most of the time. Eventually, these boys and girls begin to believe in what they have been repeating for years—that they are rotten and so is the world. In psychological terms this is called internalizing. By the age of ten

this internalizing can be complete—not a very healthy belief pattern, is it?

PREVENTION—THE KEY TO SUCCESS

If parents have a hasty, impulsive child, then early intervention is crucial for creating and stabilizing a healthy self-image. Rigorously apply the CSP. Offer praise for even small successes. Break down complex behaviors into steps (remember shaping in Chapter Five?) that the child can conquer, and then praise her for successfully taking these small steps. Give your son or daughter household responsibilities such as helping with food preparation, even if it's just pouring a can of "stuff" into a pot. Help your child feel important, confident, and independent. Show your pleasure and offer praise for her help; both mean a lot. One of my favorite parenting methods is to make positive statements about a child from an adjoining room, deliberately within earshot, so she can "overhear" the praise.

If your child makes negative statements only occasionally, let her sit on your lap and discuss her feelings. Only do this if the target behaviors of poor me's and negativeness have already been completely stopped. Then it's OK to hug, comfort, and reassure a child when she is not feeling good about herself. Tell her the many things she does well and ask her to think about these positive things.

When a poor me or a negative verbalization is rare, your offer of comfort helps a child develop a positive self-image. Just be careful that a negative verbal pattern or habit does not redevelop. When your child makes positive statements about herself, heap on the praise and the hugs.

Use the techniques outlined in this book to increase positive verbalizations, diligence in schoolwork, and responsible behaviors at home. Reinforce your kids for their successes. If you take these preventive measures, I doubt your child will ever be diagnosed as IA or HM and be placed on Ritalin.

In addition, help your children become task and emotionally independent, not tough and strong. The terms *tough* and *strong* mean being like John Wayne, that is, denying feelings or not expressing honest feelings. *Independence* means believing one can take care of oneself but still have feelings. One can be caring and sensitive and simultaneously independent. Our goal is to help our offspring develop initiative and self-confidence. Don't do everything for them; teach them to do for themselves. The more independent IA or HM children are, the more self-confident they will feel.

If your child has already been diagnosed as IA or HM, the downward spiral is probably already advanced. You must stop it immediately and completely. By this time, when children say negative things about themselves or others, they no longer know whether they mean it or are manipulating. They can't discriminate truth from manipulation.

The negative patterns must be broken by age ten. Getting all target behaviors under control, both at home and at school, is critical. You know how to do this through reinforcers and time out.

Expressing Their True Feelings

But what about IA and HM children being able to talk openly about their feelings? Parents, teachers, and psychologists may say that I have left no room for them to express themselves openly. Wrong! I *do* want them to learn to express their feelings, but I want these children to reestablish the validity and meaningfulness of what they feel. After three or four months of suppressing the poor-me's and the negative verbalizations, you can begin to let them express their feelings.

> At their first session, Jane's parents described their eight-year-old as a very emotional child. She'd cry easily if something didn't go her way. As an IA child, she was usually very quiet. If her parents or teachers tried to get her to pay attention to her schoolwork, she'd cry. She'd constantly repeat that no one loved her or that she couldn't do

anything right. The poor me's were a very important target behavior to get under control. With years of repetition Jane was beginning to feel sorry for herself and see herself as a "not OK" person, that is, she began internalizing that feeling. Under the CSP, these verbal patterns were completely stopped for four months. After that she was allowed an occasional poor me and would be comforted by her parents. We were able to reestablish her ability to discriminate between occasional periods of not feeling good about herself and seeing herself entirely as a worthless person. Remember that during those months her world changed. She began to succeed. Peers and teachers treated her better.

At times, like all of us, children get down on themselves or they don't feel well or they feel stressed out. After three or four months, we can return to putting them on our lap and discussing their feelings because now they can discern when their feelings are valid rather than manipulative.

A few nights ago, my son Kevin was looking sad and forlorn. At bedtime after prayer I jokingly said, "Good night, clone." Kevin is my double when I was his age. He then seriously asked, "Dad, did you feel like I do when you were my age?"

I said, "What do you mean, son?"

He replied, "You know, frustrated."

I asked him to explain frustrated. He then began unloading his feelings about his older brother being a good athlete and getting such good grades. I didn't try to contradict him. That would only force him to suppress these feelings. I did say that when I was his age I, too, often felt frustrated. Although I didn't have an older brother, I was close to two of my older cousins who also seemed to me to be successful at everything. Kevin lit up. I told him that as I got older I found the things I was good at, which were very different from what they were good at.

"Kevin," I said, "name some things you like to do that Alex doesn't." He replied that he was good at shortstop in baseball, whereas Alex played left field. I acknowledged this and asked for more. He said, "Well, I sing pretty well and Alex can't hum a note."

I laughed and said, "Well, that's true."

"And I like to write poems."

We then talked about his being unique and about his having his own special talents. We talked a while longer and Kevin began to sort out his feelings and realize that he was different from his brother and that indeed he was OK just being himself.

I feel that Kevin and I grew a little closer that night and that he was comfortable talking about his feelings with me. And I believe he felt a little more secure that his dad loves him for who he is while loving his brother at the same time.

THE MOST IMPORTANT THINKING PATTERN OF IA AND HM CHILDREN

The thinking or cognitive pattern of attention deficit children is central to understanding their functioning. The most fundamental cognitive or thinking pattern of these children is that they *do not think*. Behavioral approaches that endorse lots of coaching, coaxing, and prompting not only reinforce cognitive dependency but also send this message to the IA or HM child: you are incompetent, you can't think for yourself, you have a disease, and you'll need help and Ritalin for the rest of your life! Kendall and Braswell (1985) point out that IA and HM children act or react mostly emotionally instead of thinking. They don't stop to think about what behavior they are doing at the moment and how it is affecting others around them. In addition, they don't stop to think or cognitively process the consequences of their behavior.

This cognitive style was broached when we reviewed the three components of the target behavior of paying attention: looking, listening, and remembering. The failure to remember is the same as not thinking. It is crucial to understand, as I just pointed out, that the traditional way parents and teachers deal with this problem is to both inadvertently reinforce the "not thinking" and to enhance the child's belief that he can't function on his own and will always need help. In addition, failing to remember and not thinking are also closely related to the target behavior of task and cognitive dependency. This means that as long as everyone around the child is doing all the thinking for the child, he will not think.

Consider this analogy. If a man is blind or hearing-impaired, is it good to do everything for him? When you do so, things get done faster. However, the crucial point is that the man will eventually have to be able to function on his own. Conceptualize the failure to think as a problem the IA or HM child must and can overcome if he is to survive independently. Teach him that he can and must function on his own.

Make IA or HM children think! Break their pattern by carrying out the contingencies of the CSP. Reinforce your kids when they remember what to do, and put them in time out when they don't remember what to do.

Motivating the IA or HM child is of crucial importance. Talking about the importance of getting a good education, of going to college, and of aiming toward a career may be too abstract. Instead of talking, take the concrete actions we discussed in Chapter Ten about making education important.

THE IMPORTANCE OF QUIET TIME

The Bible mentions peace and serenity thousands of times, but modern children enjoy little of this. Russell Barkley has stated that hyperactive kids stay transfixed in front of video games, the television, or any activity that is excessively stimulating.

I believe that all children have become addicted to overstimulation. They watch TV from five to seven hours a day, and most of it is junk, leading to poor values. They'll play video games for hours. We overschedule them into organized athletic activities and sports lessons, music lessons, and so on. I never see children in my neighborhood going for a walk. I hardly ever see them playing out-side anymore. After one minute of quiet they'll complain, "I'm bored!" However, quiet time is important for IA and HM kids to calm down and find peace within themselves.

There are several ways to break their frenetic cycle:

1. Allow no more than one hour of junk TV, such as cartoons, a day. Completely block out stations with violent or sexual content.

2. Devote one hour every evening to family reading time. Let your children cuddle with you during this time.

3. Set aside fifteen minutes before bedtime to talk quietly. Don't use this time to lecture. In fact, be the listener.

4. Take them for a quiet walk at least once a week. Hold hands. Joke. Be playful. Teach your children the beauty and quiet of God's world.

5. Reduce organized athletics to only one sport each season, being certain it is not one that is overscheduled with too many practices or games a week.

6. Kick your children out of the house after school for an hour or two for unsupervised free play. I remember telling a former dean at the college how psychologists and cardiologists would have a lot less business if we adults played stickball, tag, football, or hopscotch (remember that game?) from 3:30 to 5:30 every afternoon.

7. Occasionally take your son or daughter to a park, a stream, or anywhere serene and teach them how to sit quietly and reflect. Remember our talk about stress? You need the quiet in your life, too. Stop the frenetic pace for your own sake as well as your child's—and do it now!

Getting IA or HM children's behavior under control helps them to win reinforcement from those around them and thus feel better about themselves. Helping them eliminate confusion between manipulative statements and true feelings avoids their developing a global and inaccurate belief about being a "not OK" person. Reassuring them and loving them give them a strong sense of self-worth. Learning to be alone with themselves and enjoy quiet time has a tremendously calming effect on their frenetic style of behavior. Put all these things together and they won't need Ritalin.

12

TEN WAYS TO STOP CREATING AN ATTENTIONAL DISORDER CHILD

$\mathbf{I}$n this chapter we're going to pull together some of the more important concepts in the Caregivers' Skills Program. We'll look at the elements that contribute to creating the IA or HM child's cognitive and behavioral patterns and at how to reverse the damage. Each misstep we cover will serve as a reminder of the solutions we've learned to the problem of keeping our children off Ritalin.

THE TEN MISSTEPS

Throughout this book I have said that no evidence confirms that attentional problems are the product of a disease or malfunction of the brain. If you are still wondering how your youngster could have gotten this way, I'll review the ten basic parenting missteps that contribute to a child's becoming IA or HM; I'll also review the solutions we've discussed.

1. *Frequent yelling at your child or other family members trains children to tune out.* A loud home trains children to not pay attention to anything.

Solution: Talk in a normal tone at all times. When telling your child to do something, speak in a calm, normal, firm tone.

2. *Frequently hitting or spanking children teaches them to tune out the discomforts of their surroundings.* It also makes them nervous and agitated, which interferes with learning and increases HM behaviors.

Solution: Use time out exactly as prescribed in this book. Use reinforcement removal when the target behavior is severe, such as aggression.

3. *Being inconsistent confuses children trying to learn right from wrong.* They don't understand when they are behaving as they should or shouldn't.

Solution: Be consistent with praise for doing things correctly and with using time out for doing things incorrectly.

4. *Doing everything for your children trains them not to think, not to problem solve, and not to be independent.* Not thinking is the key characteristic of children with attentional problems.

Solution: Use the CSP, in which the consequences require children to think, to remember, and to be attentive. Teach them to do things for themselves and to help with family responsibilities. Then require them to not only do all of these things but to remember when these tasks are to be performed.

The other day my older son wanted to call a friend but didn't have the number. He could not recall his friend's mother's first name. He did know the street but not the exact address. He asked me to look it up in the phone book. I declined, then asked him how he could track it down. He tried calling Information to see if the computer could put the last name and street name together. It couldn't. He then deduced that he had to go through all the listings for the last name and search for the street. He succeeded—not only at solving a problem but at gaining extra confidence in his thinking abilities.

Get rid of the mistaken belief that good parents wait on their children. Making them dependent makes them handicapped.

5. *Serving as your children's reminder machine teaches them how not to think for themselves.*

Solution: Use praise for remembering and time out for not remembering.

6. *Warning your children of the ramifications of their misbehavior is similar to reminding them and contributes to their not thinking.*

Solution: If they fail to do something, send them directly to time out.

7. *Sitting with your children while they do their homework teaches them dependency.*

Solution: Set up strong consequences if the school reports that a child's homework was poorly done or incomplete. Use the daily report card program. With strong enough consequences, such as loss of free play after school with no substitutions, watch how your child hustles to get schoolwork done properly.

8. *Failing to praise your children when they are behaving nicely reduces their motivation to behave correctly*—motivation to do their schoolwork and their chores, to problem solve, and to take the initiative.

Solution: IA and HM children are poorly motivated, and this can only be remedied with a high dosage of daily praise.

9. *De facto (unintentional) neglect is a prime cause of IA and HM kids.* Because we fail to train children in appropriate behavior, we fail to tenderly nurture their values and we break their spirit. Our stressful, busy lives steal from our children the quantity and quality of love and attention they need from us. The dramatic increase in the diagnosis of kids with attentional problems is not occurring because of the epidemic spread of a disease but because children without love and nurturance simply stop caring.

Solution: Carve out of your busy schedules not only quality time but sufficient time (quantity) each and every day. Children need our attention.

My friend Pete and his wonderful wife, Shirley, taught me a lesson. No matter how hectic the day, Pete and Shirley always retreated upstairs with their children at night and sat with each one, talking quietly and gently for fifteen minutes to an hour. They ended these special moments with prayer and a kiss. Their children are now enormously successful and emotionally well-balanced adults.

As a divorced father, I treasure my time with my children. When they are with me, we retreat at the end of the day to their bedroom or mine and take turns reading for a while. Kevin and Alex love humorous books. Then we chat, in the way I learned from Pete and Shirley. Finally, we kneel and say prayers, and they go to bed. I believe that if you observe this or a similar ritual 365 nights a year, beginning when the children are very young, you will no longer need my services.

10. *Failing to make education and reading important places your child at a lifelong disadvantage.* I recently had a family come to my office because their twelve-year-old daughter was not paying attention in school, was constantly gossiping with her girlfriends in class, and had only one interest—boys. Education was not an important value in her family. Why should she pay attention? Children must learn to value their education.

Solution: First, from preschool on, take a deep and sincere interest in your children's day at school. Sit and talk with them about their day and also share with them how yours went. A great time for this is dinnertime, with everyone gathered at the dining table instead of in front of the TV.

Yes, a good education is an important ingredient to getting a good job, but education in and of itself is important. If you convey excitement about your own learning as well as theirs, you'll be transmitting an important message. Time, love, attention, and interest in school, learning, and education are crucial if you want your child to pay attention and behave well in school. Remember that this is how values are taught. A child who values his education will not be diagnosed as IA or HM.

Second, offer lots of opportunities for educational enrichment. Take family visits to zoos, museums, plays, live-music concerts, historical sites, nature and science activities, and college campuses. In other words make learning new things fun, exciting, and an important family value.

Third, make reading a basic value in the family. Kids who love reading rarely display attentional problems. If you follow the ten basic ingredients we discussed earlier and use carefully what you have been taught throughout this book, wonderful changes will take place in your child. At the same time, the IA or HM (ADD or ADHD) patterns of behavior and lack of thinking disappear—*and you won't need Ritalin.*

If the problems begin to return, you are relaxing. Proper parenting to arrest and prevent attentional and misbehaving problems requires your total dedication. You must remain vigilant and work diligently for the well-being of your most loving and God-given blessing—no shortcuts.

LOVE

I want to close this book with a word from my heart as a psychologist and as a father of three children. I believe in everything I have presented in this book about the parenting skills of CSP, about IA-HM not being a disease, about the dangers of Ritalin, and about the solutions I've presented for building highly motivated and independent children. But good behavior means nothing unless we also enjoy a deep, loving relationship with our children.

I have learned from one of my favorite writers, Deepak Chopra, and from my favorite book, the Bible, that love is an unselfish thing because we give it freely and should expect nothing in return. At the same time, love is a selfish thing because it gives us so much joy, peace, and serenity in return. If the love is returned from others, it adds wonderfully to a great life. And the CSP moves our interactions with our children from anger and frustration to positive interactions and love.

Your children are precious. And now that your children are better behaved and thinking on their own, you can enjoy them so much more.

I hope that I have presented ways your child can no longer be viewed as a diseased or handicapped person but as a healthy, normal child who will henceforth reach his or her full potential and never, never, never again be put on Ritalin.

APPENDIX:
WHERE TO GET HELP—
WITHOUT MEDICATION

ORGANIZATIONS

The International Center for the Study of Psychiatry
and Psychology (ICSPP)
4628 Chestnut Street
Bethesda, MD 20814
Web site: www.icspp.org or www.breggin.com
This organization was founded and is led by Peter R. Breggin.

Parents Against Ritalin (PAR)
225 S. Brady
Claremore, OK 74017
Web site: www.p-a-r.org

Grandparents and Parents Against Ritalin (GPAR)
P.O. Box 157
Friendship, MD 20758
Web site: www.chesapeake.net/vparker/

RECOMMENDED READINGS

Talking Back to Ritalin: What Doctors Aren't Telling You About Stimulants for Children by P. R. Breggin. Monroe, ME: Common Courage Press, 1998.

The Parents' Handbook by D. Dinkmeyer, Sr., G. D. McKay, and D. Dinkmeyer, Jr. Circle Pines, MN: American Guidance Service, 1997.

How to Talk So Kids Will Listen and Listen So Kids Will Talk by A. Faber and E. Mazlish. New York: Avon, 1980.

Cognitive-Behavioral Therapy for Impulsive Children (2nd ed.) by P. C. Kendall and L. Braswell. New York: Guilford Press, 1993.

How to Deal with Difficult Discipline Problems: A Family-Systems Approach by M. Valentine. Dubuque, IA: Kendall/Hunt, 1988.

Good Kids, Bad Behavior by P. Williamson. New York: Simon & Schuster, 1990.

REFERENCES

Abramowitz, A. J., & O'Leary, S. G. (1991). Behavioral interventions for the classroom: Implications for students with ADHD. *School Psychology Review, 20,* 220–234.

Alston, C. Y., & Romney, D. M. (1992). A comparison of medicated and nonmedicated attention deficit disordered hyperactive boys. *Acta Paedopsychiatrica International Journal of Child and Adolescent Psychiatry, 55,* 65–70.

Amen, K. G., Paldi, J. H., & Thisted, R. A. (1993). Brain SPECT imaging. *Journal of the American Academy of Child and Adolescent Psychiatry, 32,* 1080–1081.

American Psychiatric Association. (1994). *Diagnostic and statistical manual of mental disorders* (4th ed.). Washington, DC: Author.

Arnold, L. E., Kleykamp, K., Votolato, N., & Gibson, R. A. (1994). Potential link between dietary intake of fatty acids and behavior: Pilot exploration of serum lipids in attention deficit hyperactivity disorder. *Journal of Child and Adolescent Psychopharmacology, 4,* 171–182.

Auci, D. L. (1997). Methylphenidate and the immune system. *Journal of the American Academy of Child and Adolescent Psychiatry, 36,* 1015–1016.

Axelrod, S. (1974). *Behavior modification for the classroom teacher.* New York: McGraw-Hill.

Balthazor, M. J., Wagner, R. K., & Pelham, W. E. (1991). The specificity of the effects of stimulant medication on classroom learning-related measures of cognitive processing for attention deficit disorder children. *Journal of Abnormal Child Psychology, 19,* 35–52.

Barkley, R. A. (1981). *Hyperactive children: A handbook for diagnosis and treatment.* New York: Guilford Press.

Barkley, R. A. (1987). *Defiant children: A clinician's manual for parent training.* New York: Guilford Press.

Barkley, R. A. (1990). *ADHD: A handbook for diagnosis and treatment.* New York: Guilford Press.

Barkley, R. A. (1991). Attention deficit hyperactivity disorder. *Psychiatric Annals, 21,* 725–733.

Barkley, R. A. (1992a). *ADHD: What can we do?* New York: Guilford Press (video).

Barkley, R. A. (1992b). *ADHD: What do we know?* New York: Guilford Press (video).

Barkley, R. A. (1995). *Taking charge of ADHD: The complete authoritative guide for parents.* Nebraska: Boys Town Press.

Beck, A. (1988). *Love is never enough.* New York: HarperCollins.

Becker, W. C. (1971). *Parents are teachers: A child management program.* Champaign, IL: Research Press.

Berkow, R., & Beers, M., Editors. (1997). *The Merck manual of medical information: Home edition.* Rahway, NJ: Merck Research Laboratories.

Berne, E. (1964). *Games people play.* New York: Grove Press.

Blackman, J. A., Westervelt, V. D., Stevenson, R., & Welch, A. (1991). Management of preschool children with attention deficit hyperactivity disorder. *Topics in Early Childhood Special Education, 1*(1), 91–104.

Block, M. A. (1996). *No more Ritalin: Treating ADHD without drugs.* New York: Kensington Books.

Braswell, L., & Bloomquist, M. (1991). *Cognitive-behavioral therapy with ADHD children: Child, family, and school intervention.* New York: Guilford Press.

Braughman, F. A. (1997, August 6). Drugging normal kids. *The Farmville Herald,* pp. 1–2.

Breggin, G. R., & Breggin, P. R. (1995). The hazards of treating "attention deficit hyperactivity disorder" with methylphenidate (Ritalin). *Journal of College Student Psychotherapy, 10*(2), 55–72.

Breggin, P. R. (1998). *Talking back to Ritalin: What doctors aren't telling you about stimulants for children.* Monroe, ME: Common Courage Press.

Brooks, R. (1991). *The self-esteem teacher*. Circle Pines, MN: American Guidance Service.

Brown, D. G. (1972). *Behavior modification in children, school and family*. Champaign, IL: Research Press.

Busch, B. (1993). Attention deficits: Current concepts, controversies, management, and approaches to classroom instruction. *Annals of Dyslexia, 43*, 5–25.

Capute, A., Neidermeyer, F., & Richardson, F. (1974). The electroencephalogram in children with minimal cerebral dysfunction. *Pediatrics, 41*(1), 104–111, 114.

Carlson, C. L., & Bunner, M. R. (1993). Effects of methylphenidate on the academic performance of children with ADHD and learning disabilities. *School Psychology Review, 22*, 184–198.

Carlson, C. L., Pelham, W. E., Milich, R., & Dixon, J. (1992). Single and combined effects of methylphenidate and behavior therapy on the classroom performance of children with attention deficit hyperactivity disorder. *Journal of Abnormal Child Psychology, 20*, 213–232.

Castellanos, F. X., Giedd, J. N., Eckburg, P., Marsh, W. L., Vaituzis, C., Kaysen, D., Hamburger, S. D., & Rapoport, J. (1994). Quantitative morphology of the caudate nucleus in attention deficit hyperactivity disorder. *American Journal of Psychiatry, 151*, 1791–1796.

Chopra, D. (1993). *Ageless body, timeless mind*. New York: Random House.

Clements, S. D., & Peters, J. (1962). Minimal brain dysfunction in the school-age child. *Archives of General Psychiatry, 6*, 185–197.

Danforth, J. S., Barkley, R. A., & Stokes, T. F. (1991). Observations of parent-child interactions with hyperactive children: Research and clinical implications. *Clinical Psychology Review, 11*, 703–727.

Davison, L. C., & Neal, J. M. (1994). *Abnormal psychology* (6th ed.). New York: Wiley.

DeRisi, W. J., & Butz, G. (1975). *Writing behavioral contracts: A case simulation and practice manual*. Champaign, IL: Research Press.

DiTraglia, J. (1991). Methylphenidate protocol: Feasibility in a pediatric practice. *Clinical Pediatrics, 30*, 656–660.

Dobson, J. (1978). *The strong-willed child*. Wheaton, IL: Tyndale House.

Drug Enforcement Administration. (1996, December 10–12). *Conference report: Stimulants use in the treatment of ADHD*. Washington, DC: DEA/U.S. Department of Justice.

DuPaul, G. J. (1991). Attention deficit hyperactivity disorder: Classroom intervention strategies. *School Psychology International, 12*, 85–94.

DuPaul, G. J., & Barkley, R. A. (1993). Behavioral contributions to pharmacotherapy: The utility of behavioral methodology in medication
treatment of children with ADHD. *Behavior Therapy, 24,* 47–65.

DuPaul, G. J., Barkley, R. A., & McMurray, M. B. (1991). Therapeutic effects
of medication on ADHD: Implications for school psychologists. *School
Psychology Review, 20,* 203–219.

DuPaul, G. J., Guevremont, D. C., & Barkley, R. A. (1992). Behavioral treatment of attention deficit hyperactivity disorder in the classroom: The
use of attention training system. *Behavior Modification, 16,* 204–225.

Durkheim, E. (1912). *The elementary focus of religious life.* New York: Macmillan.

Erk, R. R. (1995). The conundrum of attention deficit disorder. *Journal of Mental
Health Counseling, 17,* 131–145.

Ernst, K. M., Liebenauer, L., King, A. C., & Gitzgerald, G. A. (1994). Reduced
brain metabolism in hyperactive girls. *Journal of the American Academy of
Child and Adolescent Psychiatry, 33,* 858–868.

Ernst, K. M., Zametkin, A. J., Matochik, J. A., & Liebenauer, L. (1994). Effects
of intravenous dextroamphetamine on brain metabolism in adults with
attention deficit hyperactivity disorder. *Psychopharmacology Bulletin, 30,*
219–225.

Feld, S. L. (1991). Why your friends have more friends than you do. *American
Journal of Sociology, 96(C)(1),* 464–1477.

Finn, J. D., Achilles, C., Bain, H., & Folger, J. (1990). Three years in a small
class. *Teaching and Teacher Education, 6(2),* 127–136.

Fowler, M. (1993). *CH.A.D.D. educators manual: an in-depth look at attention
deficit disorders from an educational perspective.* Plantation, FL: CH.A.D.D.

Fowler, M. (1993). *Maybe you know my kid.* New York: Carol.

France, K. G. (1993). Management of infant sleep disturbance: A review.
Clinical Psychology Review, 13, 635–647.

Fromm, E. (1956). *The art of loving.* New York: HarperCollins.

Garber, S. W., Garber, M. D., & Spezman, R. F. (1996). *Beyond Ritalin: Facts
about medication and other strategies for helping children, adolescents, and
adults with attention deficit disorders.* New York: Harper Perennial.

Ghosh, S., & Chattopadhyay, P. K. (1993). Application of behavior modification techniques in treatment of attention deficit hyperactivity disorder:
A case report. *Indian Journal of Clinical Psychology, 20,* 124–129.

Gibson, W. (1957). *The miracle worker: A play for television.* New York: Knots.

Giedd, J. N., Castellanos, F. X., Casey, B. J., Kozuch, P., King, C., Hamburger, S.,
& Rapoport, J. (1994). Quantitative morphology of the corpus callosum
in attention deficit hyperactivity disorder. *American Journal of Psychiatry,
151,* 665–669.

Glasser, W. (1965). *Reality therapy: A new approach to psychiatry*. New York: HarperCollins.

Golden, G. S. (1974). Gilles de la Tourette's Syndrome following methylphenidate administration. *Developmental Medicine and Child Neurology, 16,* 76–78.

Goldstein, S., & Goldstein, M. (1989). *Why won't my child pay attention?* UT: Neurology, Learning and Behavior Center (video).

Goldstein, S., & Goldstein, M. (1990). *Educating inattentive children*. UT: Neurology, Learning and Behavior Center (video).

Goldstein, S., & Goldstein, M. (1992). *Hyperactivity: Why won't my child pay attention?* New York: Wiley.

Gordon, M. (1991). *ADHD/Hyperactivity: A consumer's guide*. New York: GSI Publications.

Gordon, M., Thomason, D., Cooper, S., & Ivers, C. L. (1991). Nonmedical treatment of ADHD/hyperactivity: The attention training system. *Journal of School Psychology, 29,* 151–159.

Gordon, T. (1970). *P.E.T. Parent effectiveness training: The tested new way to raise responsible children*. New York: Peter H. Wyden.

Graziano, A. M., & Namaste, K. A. (1990). Parental use of physical force in child discipline: A survey of 679 college students. *Journal of Interpersonal Violence, 5,* 449–463.

Greenberg, G., & Horn, W. (1991). *ADHD: Questions and answers*. Champaign, IL: Research Press.

Greenblatt, J. M., Huffman, L. C., & Reiss, A. L. (1994). Folic acid in neurodevelopment and child psychiatry. *Progress in Neuropsychopharmacology and Biological Psychiatry, 18,* 647–660.

Greenhill, L. L. (1989). Treatment issues in children with attention deficit hyperactivity disorder. *Psychiatric Annals, 19,* 604–613.

Gross, M. B., & Wilson, W. C. (1974). Intelligence, academic achievement and EEG abnormalities in hyperactive children. *American Journal of Psychiatry, 131,* 391–395. In I. B. Weiner (1992), *Child and adolescent psychopathology*. New York: Wiley.

Guffey, D. G. (1992). Ritalin: What educators and parents should know. *Journal of Instructional Psychology, 19,* 167–169.

Gullo, D. F., & Burton, G. B. (1992). The effects of social class, class size, and prekindergarten experience on early school adjustment. American Educational Research Conference, San Francisco.

Hallowell, E. M., & Rutey, J. J. (1994). *Driven to distraction: Recognizing and coping with attention deficit disorder from childhood through adulthood*. New York: Pantheon Press.

Harris, T. (1969). *I'm OK—You're OK: A practical guide to transactional analysis.* New York: HarperCollins.

Heilman, K. M., Voeller, K. K., & Nadeau, S. E. (1991). A possible pathophysiologic substrate of attention deficit hyperactivity disorder. *Journal of Child Neurology, 6,* S76–S81.

Hetchman, L. (1986). Attention deficit disorder. *Current Pediatric Therapy, 12,* 21–23.

Horn, W. F., Ialongo, N. S., Pascoe, J. M., & Greenberg, G. (1991). Additive effects of psychostimulants, parent training, and self-control therapy with ADHD children. *Journal of the American Academy of Child and Adolescent Psychiatry, 30,* 233–240.

Houlihan, M., & VanHouten, R. (1989). Behavioral treatment of hyperactivity: A review and overview. *Education and Treatment of Children, 12,* 265–275.

Hunter, D. (1995). *The Ritalin-free child: Managing hyperactivity and attention deficits without drugs.* Ft. Lauderdale, FL: Consumer Press.

Ialongo, N. S., Lopez, M., Horn, W. F., & Pascoe, J. M. (1994). Effects of psychostimulant medication on self-perceptions of competence, control, and mood in children with ADHD. *Journal of Clinical Child Psychology, 23,* 161–173.

Ingersoll, B. (1988). *Your hyperactive child: A parent's guide to coping with attention deficit disorder.* New York: Doubleday.

Ingersoll, B., & Goldstein, S. (1993). *Attention deficit disorder and learning disabilities: Realities, myths and controversial treatments.* New York: Bantam Doubleday Dell.

International Narcotics Board. (1996). *Report for 1996.* (United Nations Publications No. E.97XI.3). Vienna, Austria: Author.

Jensen, G. D., & Womack, M. G. (1967). Operant conditioning techniques applied in the treatment of an autistic child. *American Journal of Orthopsychiatry, 37,* 30–34.

Jensen, L. L., & Kington, M. (1986). *Parenting.* Austin, TX: Holt, Rinehart and Winston.

Johnson, C. M., Yehl, J. F., & Stack, J. M. (1989). Compliance training in a child with attention deficit hyperactivity disorder: A case study. *Family Practice Research Journal, 9,* 73–80.

Johnson, D. J., & Myklebust, H. R. (1967). *Learning disabilities: Educational principles and practices.* New York: Grune & Stratton.

Johnston, C., & Finem, S. (1993). Methods of evaluating methylphenidate in children with ADHD: Acceptability, satisfaction and compliance. *Journal of Pediatric Psychology, 18,* 717–730.

Jung, C. (1928). *Contributions to analytical psychology*. Orlando, FL: Harcourt Brace.

Kelly, K., & Ramundo, P. (1992). *You mean I'm not lazy, stupid or crazy?!* New York: Scribner.

Kendall, P. C. (1996) *Cognitive therapy with children*. Workshop presented in Richmond, Virginia.

Kendall, P. C., & Braswell, L. (1982). Cognitive-behavioral self-control therapy for children: A components analysis. *Journal of Consulting and Clinical Psychology, 50,* 672–690.

Kendall, P. C., & Braswell, L. (1985). *Cognitive-behavioral therapy for impulsive children*. New York: Guilford Press.

Kendall, P. C., & Braswell, L. (1993). *Cognitive-behavioral therapy for impulsive children* (2nd ed.). New York: Guilford Press.

Kendall, P. C., & Raber, M. (1987). Reply to Abickoff and Gittelman's evaluation of cognitive training with medicated hyperactive children. *Archives of General Psychiatry, 8,* 77–79.

Kesler, J. W. (1988). *Psychopathology of childhood* (2nd ed.). Englewood Cliffs, NJ: Prentice Hall.

Klorman, R., Brumaghim, J. T., Fitzpatrick, P. A., & Borgstedt, A. D. (1994). Clinical and cognitive effects of methylphenidate on children with ADD as a function of aggression/oppositionality and age. *Journal of Abnormal Psychology, 103,* 206–221.

Lader, M. (1983). *Introduction to psychopharmacology*. MI: Upjohn.

Lahat, E., Avital, E., Barr, J., Berkovitch, M., Arlazoroff, A., & Aladjem, M. (1995). BAEP studies in children with attention deficit disorder. *Developmental Medicine and Child Neurology, 37,* 119–123.

Larzelere, R. E. (1993). Response to Oosterhuis: Empirically justified uses of spanking: Toward a discriminating view of corporal punishment. *Journal of Psychology and Theology, 21,* 142–147.

Latham, P. S., & Latham, P. H. (1993). *Attention deficit disorder and the law*. Washington, DC: JKL Communications.

Levine, D. (Ed.). (1965). *Nebraska symposium on modification*. Lincoln: University of Nebraska Press.

Levy, F. (1989). CNS stimulant controversies. *Australian and New Zealand Journal of Psychiatry, 23,* 497–502.

Levy, F. (1991). The dopamine theory of attention deficit hyperactivity disorder. *Australian and New Zealand Journal of Psychiatry, 25,* 277–283.

Lewinsohn, P. M., & Rosenbaum, M. (1987). Recall of parental behavior by acute depressives, remitted depressives, and nondepressives. *Journal of Personality and Social Psychology, 52*(3), 611–619.

Lucker, J. R., & Molloy, A. T. (1995). Resource for working with children with attention deficit/hyperactivity disorder. *Elementary School Guidance and Counseling, 29,* 260–277.

Malone, M. A., & Swanson, J. M. (1993). Effects of methylphenidate on impulsive responding in children with ADHD. *Journal of Child Neurology, 8,* 157–163.

Martin, G., & Pear, J. (1988). *Behavioral modification: What it is and how to do it* (3rd ed.). Englewood Cliffs, NJ: Prentice Hall.

Maslow, A.H. (1962). *Toward a psychology of being.* New York: Van Nostrand.

Mathieu, J. F., Ferron, A., Dewar, K. M., & Reader, T. A. (1989). Acute and chronic effects of methylphenidate on cortical adrenoreceptors in the rat. *European Journal of Pharmacology, 162,* 173–178.

Matier, K., Halperin, J. M., & Sharma, V. (1992). Methylphenidate response in aggressive and nonaggressive ADHD children: Distinctions on laboratory measures of symptoms. *Journal of the American Academy of Child and Adolescent Psychiatry, 31,* 219–225.

Matochik, J. A., Liebenauer, L. L., King, A. C., & Szymanski, H. V. (1994). Cerebral glucose metabolism in adults with attention deficit hyperactivity disorder after chronic stimulant treatment. *American Journal of Psychiatry, 151,* 658–664.

Mayberg, H. (1998, May 27). *Today.* New York: National Broadcasting Network.

McCain, A. P., & Kelley, M. L. (1993). Managing the classroom behavior of an ADHD preschooler: The efficacy of a school-home note intervention. *Child and Family Behavior Therapy, 15,* 33–44.

Miller, A. R. (1992). ADHD and research methodology. *Journal of the American Academy of Child and Adolescent Psychiatry, 31,* 17–172.

Miller, D. L., & Kelley, M. L. (1992). Treatment acceptability: The effects of parent gender, marital adjustment, and child behavior. *Child and Family Behavior Therapy, 14,* 11–23.

Mischel, W. (1968). *Personality and assessment.* New York: Wiley.

Molchan, S. E., Sunderland, T., Matochik, J. A., & Zametkin, A. J. (1995). Effects of scopolamine on human brain glucose consumption. *Neuropsychopharmacology, 12,* 175–276.

Moore, T. (1992). *Care of the soul.* New York: HarperCollins.

Nasrallah, H., Loney, J., Olsen, S., McCalley-Whitters, M., Kramer, J., & Jacoby, C. (1986). Cortical atrophy in young adults with a history of hyperactivity in childhood. *Psychiatry Research, 17,* 241–246.

Nathan, W. A. (1992). Integrated multimodal therapy of children with attention deficit hyperactivity disorder. *Bulletin of the Menninger Clinic, 56,* 283–312.

Newby, R. F. (1996). Parent training for children with attention-deficit/ hyperactivity disorder. In *The Hatherleigh guide to psychiatric disorder* (pp. 191–220). New York: Hatherleigh Press.

Palmer, P. J. (1998). *The courage to teach: Exploring the inner landscape of a teacher's life*. San Francisco: Jossey-Bass.

Parker, H. (1992). *The ADAPT program*. Plantation, FL: Specialty Press.

Parker, H. (1992). *The ADD hyperactivity handbook for schools*. Plantation, FL: Specialty Press.

Parker, H. (1994). *The ADD hyperactivity workbook for parents, teachers, and kids*. Plantation, FL: Specialty Press.

Parker, H. (1990). *Listen, look and think*. Plantation, FL: Specialty Press.

Parker, H. (1991). *The goal card program*. Plantation, FL: Specialty Press.

Patterson, G. R. (1971). *Families: Applications of social learning to family life*. Champaign, IL: Research Press.

Patterson, G. R. (1968). *Living with children: New methods for parents and teachers*. Champaign, IL: Research Press.

Pelham, W. E. (1993). Pharmacotherapy for children with ADHD. *School Psychology Review, 22,* 199–227.

Pelham, W. E., Carlson, C. L., Sams, S. E., & Vallano, G. (1993). Separate AND combined effects of methylphenidate and behavior modification on boys with ADHD in the classroom. *Journal of Consulting and Clinical Psychology, 61,* 506–515.

Pelham, W. E., Murphy, D. A., Vannatta, K., & Milich, R. (1993). Methylphenidate and attributions in boys with ADHS. *Annual Progress in Child Psychiatry and Child Development,* 242–265.

Phelan, T. (1984). *All about attention deficit disorder*. Glen Ellyn, IL: Child Management.

Phelan, T. (1984). *All about attention deficit disorder*. Glen Ellyn, IL: Child Management (video).

Phelan, T. (1984). *1-2-3 magic! Training your preschoolers and preteens to do what you want*. Glen Ellyn, IL: Child Management (video).

Phelan, T. (1991). *Surviving your adolescents*. Glen Ellyn, IL: Child Management.

Physicians' Desk Reference. (1997). Oradell, NJ: Medical Economics Co.

Pitts, C. E. (1971). *Operant conditioning in the classroom*. New York: Crowell.

Premack, D. (1965). Reinforcement theory. In D. Levine (ed.), Nebraska Symposium on Motivation, *29,* 123–188. Lincoln: University of Nebraska Press.

Quay, H. C., & Werry, J. S. (1986). *Psychopathological disorders of childhood* (3rd ed.). New York: Wiley.

Rao, J. K., Julius, J. R., Blethen, T. J., & Breen, T. J. (1997). Idiopathic growth hormone deficiency and attention deficit disorder (ADD): Effect of methylphenidate and pemoline on GH therapy: The National Cooperative Growth Study Results.

Reichenberg-Ullman, J., & Ullman, R. (1996). *Ritalin-free kids: Safe and effective homeopathic medicine for ADD and other behavioral and learning problems.* Rocklin, CA: Prima.

Rief, S. (1993). *How to reach and teach ADD/ADHD children.* New York: Center for Applied Research in Education.

Rogers, C. R. (1951). *Client-centered therapy: Its current practice, implications, and theory.* Boston: Houghton Mifflin.

Rubin, N. (1989, February). The truth about creativity. *Parents, 64,* 111–112.

Sarason, I. G., & Sarason, B. R. (1989). *Abnormal psychology* (6th ed.). Englewood Cliffs, NJ: Prentice Hall.

Satterfield, J., Cantwell, D., Saul, R., & Yusin, A. (1974). *Minimal brain dysfunction: A clinical study on incidence, diagnosis and treatment in over 1,000 children.* New York: Brunner/Mazel.

Schwartz, S., & Johnson, J. H. (1985). *Psychopathology of childhood: A clinical-experimental approach* (2nd ed.). New York: Pergamon.

Sedvall, G. (1992). The current status of PET scanning with respect to schizophrenia. *Neuropsychopharmacology, 7*(1), 41–54.

Seligman, L. (1995). *DSM-IV: Diagnosis and treatment planning.* Virginia: American Counseling Association (audiotape).

Selye, H. (1976). *The stress of life.* New York: McGraw-Hill.

Shue, K. L., & Douglas, V. I. (1992). Attention deficit hyperactivity disorder and the frontal lobe syndrome. *Brain and Cognition, 20,* 104–124.

Silver, L. (1993). *Dr. Larry Silver's advice to parents on attention-deficit hyperactivity disorder.* Washington, DC: American Psychiatric Press.

Silver, L. (1984). *The misunderstood child: A guide for parents of LD children.* New York: McGraw-Hill.

Silverman, H. M., & Simon, G. I. (1992). *The pill book* (5th ed.). New York: Bantam.

Silverstein, J. M., & Allison, D. B. (1994). The comparative efficacy of antecedent exercise and methylphenidate: A single case randomized trial. *Child Care, Health and Development, 20,* 47–60.

Solanto, M. V. (1990). Increasing difficulties with age in ADHD children. *Journal of Developmental and Behavioral Pediatrics, 11,* 27.

Stein, D. B. (1990). *Controlling the difficult adolescent: The REST program (the Real Economy System for Teens).* Lanham, MD: University Press of America.

Steiner, C. M. (1974). *Scripts people live.* New York: Random House.

Still, G. F. (1902). The Coulstonian lectures on some abnormal physical conditions in children. *Lancet, 1,* 1008–1082.

Strassberg, Z., Dodge, K. A., Pettit, G. S., & Bates, J. E. (1994). Spanking in the home and children's subsequent aggression toward kindergarten peers. *Development and Psychopathology, 6a,* 445–461.

Straus, A., & Lehtiner, L. W. (1947). Psychopathology and education of the brain impaired child. New York: Grune & Stratton.

Swanson, J. M., McBurnett, K., Wigal, T., & Pfiffner, L. J. (1993). Effect of stimulant medication on children with ADD: A review of reviews. *Exceptional Children, 60,* 154–161.

Taylor, M. J., Voros, J. G., Logan, W. J., & Malone, M. A. (1993). Changes in event-related potentials with stimulant medication in children with ADHD. *Biological Psychology, 36,* 139–156.

Thoreau, H. D. (1854). *Walden: Life in the woods.* Boston: Tichnor & Fields.

van Bilsen, H., Kendall, P. C., & Slavenburg, J. H. (1995). *Behavioral approaches for children and adolescents: Challenges for the next century.* New York: Plenum.

van der Vlugt, H., Pijenburg, H. M., Wels, P.M.A., & Konig, A. (1995). Cognitive behavior modification of ADHD: A family system approach. In H. van Bilsen, P. C. Kendall, and J. H. Slavenburg, *Behavioral approaches for children and adolescents: Challenges for the next century* (pp. 67–75). New York: Plenum.

Weber, K. S., Frakenberger, W., & Heilman, K. (1992). The effects of Ritalin on the academic achievement of children diagnosed with attention deficit hyperactivity disorder. *Developmental Disabilities Bulletin, 20,* 49–68.

Webster-Stratton, C. (1990). Enhancing the effectiveness of self-administered videotape parent training for families with conduct-problem children. *Journal of Abnormal Child Psychology, 18,* 479–492.

Weil, A. M., & Rosen, W. (1983). *Chocolate to morphine: Understanding mind-active drugs.* Boston: Houghton Mifflin.

Weiner, I. B. (1982). *Child and adolescent psychopathology.* New York: Wiley.

Weiss, L. (1992). *Attention deficit disorder in adults.* Dallas, TX: Taylor.

Wenar, C. (1994). *Developmental psychopathology: From infancy through adolescence* (3rd ed.). New York: McGraw-Hill.

Wender, P. H. (1987). *The hyperactive child, adolescent, and adult: Attention deficit disorder through the life span.* New York: Oxford University Press.

Whalen C. K., & Henker, B. (1991). Therapies for hyperactive children: Comparisons, combinations, & compromises. *Journal of Consulting & Clinical Psychology, 59,* 126–137.

Wilens, T. E., & Biederman, J. (1992). The stimulants. *Pediatric Psychopharmacology, 15*, 191–222.

Witters, W., Venturelli, P., & Hanson, G. (1992). *Drugs and society* (3rd ed.). Boston: Jones & Bartlett.

Wright, J. W. (1997). *Do we really need Ritalin?: A family guide to attention deficit hyperactivity disorder (ADHD)*. New York: Avon.

Wright, L. (1978). *Parentpower*. New York: Psychological Dimensions.

Yudolsky, S. C., Hales, R. E., & Ferguson, T. (1991). *What YOU need to know about psychiatric drugs*. New York: Ballantine.

Zametkin, A. J., Liebenauer, L. L., Gitzgerald, G. A., & King, A. C. (1993). Brain metabolism in teenagers with attention deficit hyperactivity disorder. *Archives of General Psychiatry, 50*, 333–340.

Zimbardo, P. G. (1977). *Shyness, what it is, what to do about it*. Reading, MA: Addison-Wesley.

Zimbardo, P. G., & Radl, S. (1981). *The shy child*. New York: McGraw-Hill.

THE AUTHOR

David B. Stein received his bachelor's degree from the City University of New York, Brooklyn College, and his master's and doctoral degrees from Virginia Commonwealth University. There he served as the university's president of Psi Chi—the national honor society for psychology. He completed his residency at the University of Mississippi Medical Center.

Stein is associate professor of psychology at Longwood College, which is part of the Virginia state college system. He has been an educator, writer, speaker, and practitioner for over twenty-five years and has taught at the elementary, intermediate, college, and graduate school levels. He is a former clinical assistant professor of psychiatry at the University of Tennessee Center for the Health Sciences. His clinical experiences include being a staff psychologist at the Memphis Mental Health Institute, director of psychological services at a home for adolescents, a staff psychologist at mental health centers, and owner and director of a private psychology treatment center in Memphis.

Stein is listed in *Who's Who Among America's Teachers, 1998*, and *Outstanding Americans, 1998*. He is a member of the Council for the National Register of Health Service Providers in Psychology. He is credited in *National Contributions to Mental Health* with developing the first divorce recovery therapy group in the South.

He is licensed as a clinical psychologist in Virginia and Tennessee and as a school psychologist in New York.

Stein authored the first book on comprehensive behavioral treatment strategies for oppositional and defiant adolescents, titled *Controlling the Difficult Adolescent: The REST Program (Real Economy System for Teens)* (1990).

INDEX

191